Music Theory for Singers

Level Three

Second Edition

Sarah Sandvig

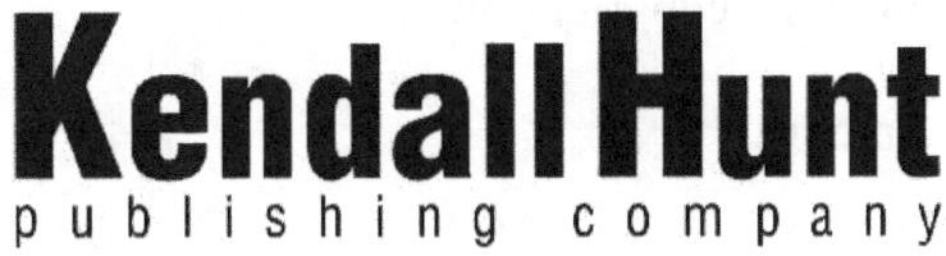

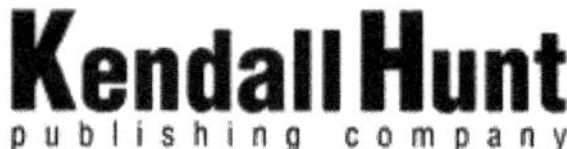

www.kendallhunt.com
Send all inquiries to:
4050 Westmark Drive
Dubuque, IA 52004-1840

ISBN 978-1-5249-1438-7

Published in the United States of America

FOREWORD

In Sarah Sandvig's *Music Theory for Singers*, voice students and their teachers finally have a singer-friendly primer for musicianship and music theory that is directly applicable to voice training. Mrs. Sandvig has capitalized on her experience as a successful private voice teacher to create this comprehensive workbook, which, in clear, concise language, lays out an easy-to-follow lesson plan progressing from basic through advanced skills. *Music Theory for Singers* is equally applicable in a college or high school classroom setting as in the private studio, and voice teachers will especially appreciate the inclusion of international musical terminology, and music history which their students are likely to encounter in vocal repertoire. For teens studying voice for the first time, as well as for life-long adult singers, *Music Theory for Singers* will become a valued adjunct to any level of vocal study.

Juliana Gondek
Metropolitan Opera soloist and
Prize-winning international recording artist
Professor and Chair, Division of Voice Studies
UCLA

I am beginning my first semester as a BFA Musical Theatre Major at The Boston Conservatory at Berklee. I used Sarah's theory books throughout high school from levels 5 through 10, and they have prepared me immensely for this first semester – and beyond. For example, I recently went through a music theory and sight singing placement test: I was so amazed how comfortable I felt with both the written and singing portions. It was everything I had already learned from these theory books – key signatures, scales, rhythm, solfege, and more. In addition, I became so familiar with the fundamentals of music and a piano keyboard (even through utilizing the vocal theory books) I was able to test out of a whole year of beginner piano. All of this creates the possibility for me to move on to higher levels and be more challenged than if I had to start from the basics. Not to mention all of the composers and terms that are necessary knowledge to be successful in professional music classes and settings. It feels good to know that if I am ever unsure about what I am learning in class, my theory books are right there on the bookshelf to help me out.

Sofia Ross
Musical Theatre Major
Boston Conservatory

Thank you to the following people for their help and guidance in writing these books: Mary Beard, Melissa Caldretti, Sally Curry, Sharlae Jenkins, Vanessa Parvin, Connie Venti & my dad, Ken Watson.

Thank you to my husband Darren and sons Aiden & Caleb for their love, support and patience throughout this writing process.

NOTE TO TEACHER:
These books are a supplement to private, group or classroom voice lessons, and though I feel they can stand alone, they are not meant as a replacement for a good teacher who ensures student learning and understanding of music theory, history, and sight-singing. Each book includes reviews of subjects with a review test (with answers) at the end. You may also purchase the Answer Key, which has answers to all pages in each level, 1-10. Composers, terms, IPA and solfege are unique elements of these books that make them especially helpful for singers.

I hope these books are a useful addition to the many tools you already utilize to teach young singers in your studio or classroom.

TABLE OF CONTENTS

MUSIC THEORY FOR SINGERS

LEVEL 3

Review of Concepts in Level 2

The Staff: Review

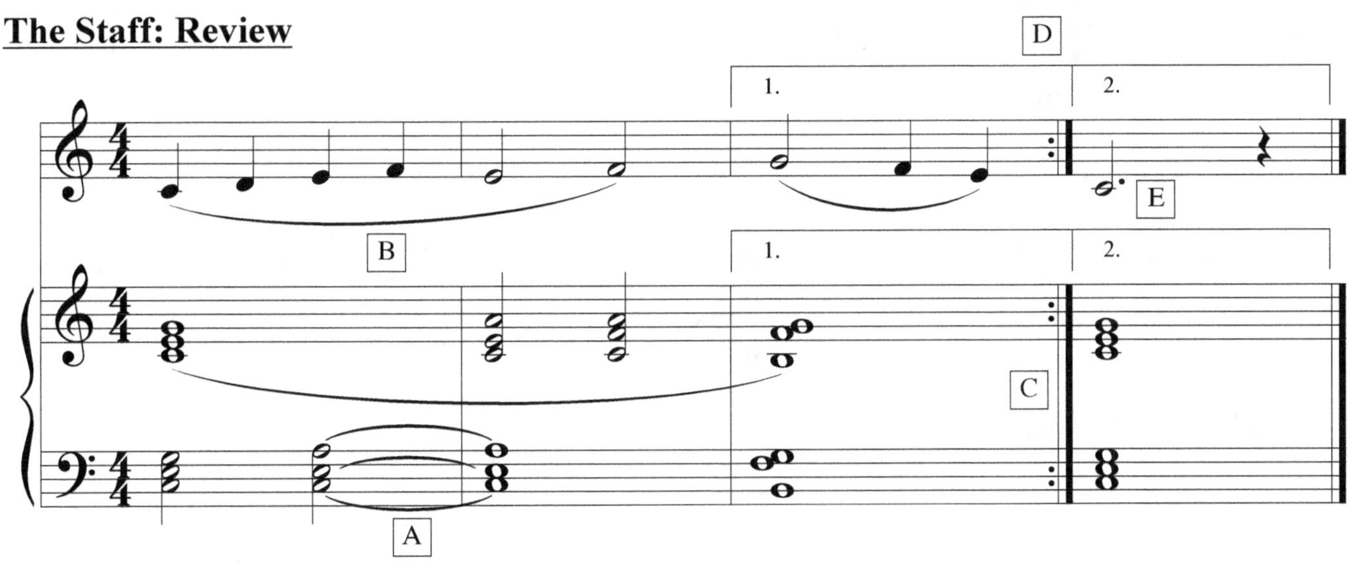

A. Tie

B. Slur

C. Repeat Signs

D. 1st & 2nd Endings

E. Dotted Half Note

Notes, Rhythm & Time Signtaure: Review

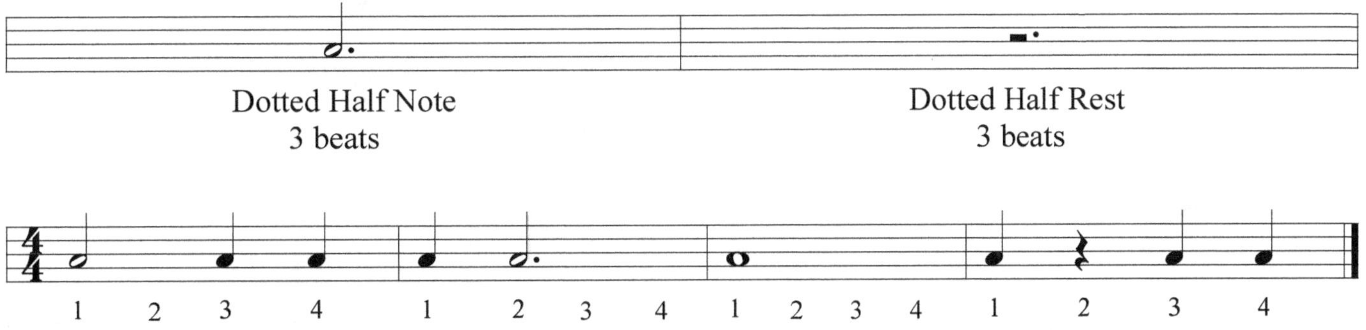

Note Review: Ledger Lines

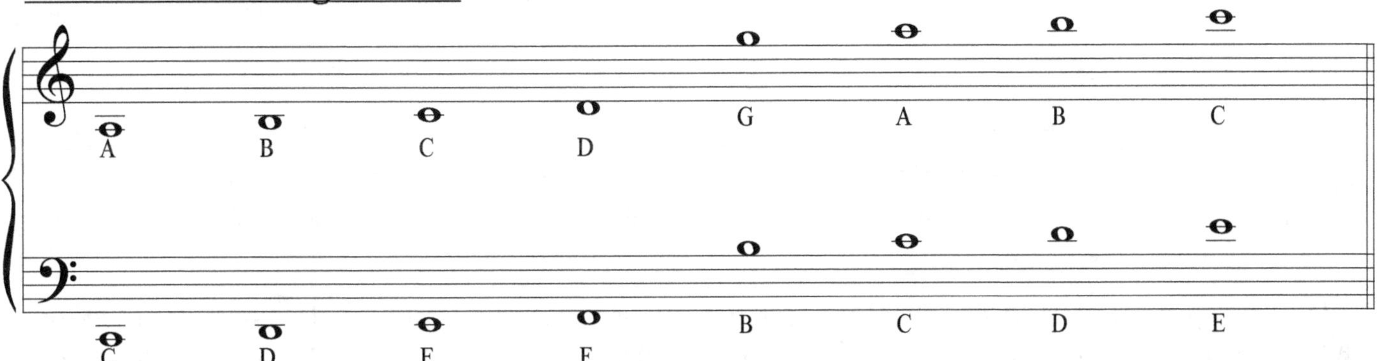

Key Signature & Triad Review

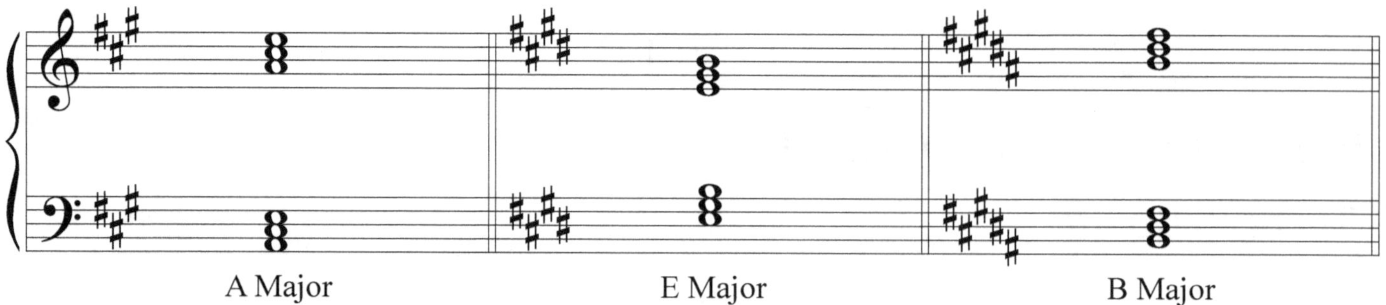

Interval Review

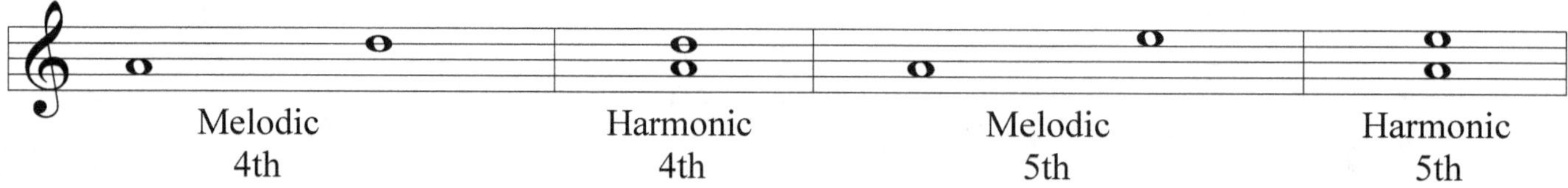

IPA/Diction Review

IPA SYMBOL	SOUND IN ENGLISH WORD	IPA SPELLING OF WORD	TONGUE/LIPS PLACEMENT
i	ski	[ski]	Center of tongue is high Lips relaxed
ɛ	led	[lɛd]	Low tongue Lips relaxed
ɑ	father	[ˈfɑðər]	Low tongue Lips relaxed
o	obey	[oʊˈbeɪ]	Low tongue, tip behind bottom teeth Rounded lips
u	goose	[gus]	Low tongue, tip behind bottom teeth Rounded lips
ɪ	kit	[kɪt]	High tongue, sides touching top teeth Lips relaxed
e	ate	[eɪt]	High tongue, sides touching top teeth Lips relaxed
ə	afraid	[əˈfreɪd]	Mid tongue, tip behind bottom teeth Lips relaxed

Sight-singing Review

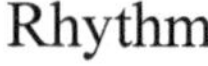
Rhythm

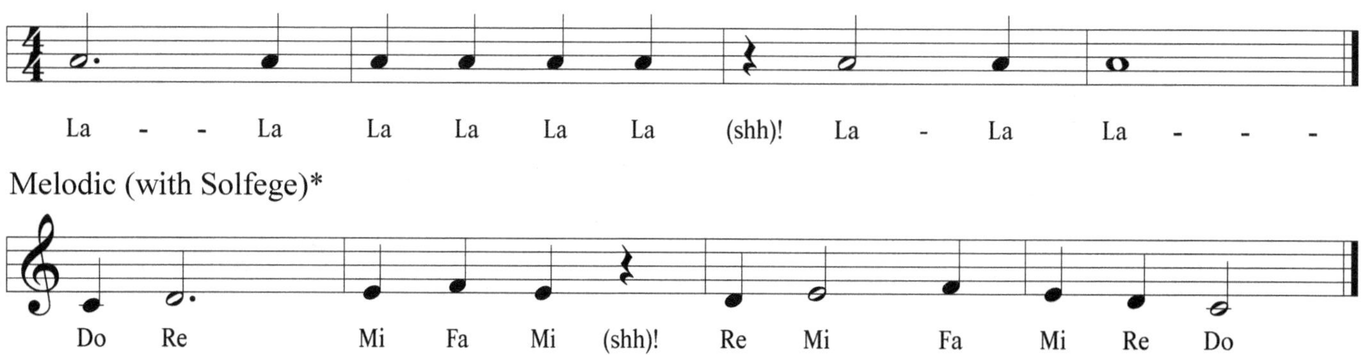

*The Solfege system assigns a syllable to each note of a scale starting with Do. The syllables used for a major scale are: Do Re Mi Fa Sol La Ti Do. Solfege has been in existence for more than 1,000 years!

Lesson 1: The Natural Sign

A Natural Sign (♮) cancels an added accidental (♯/♭) in music. Look at the example below.

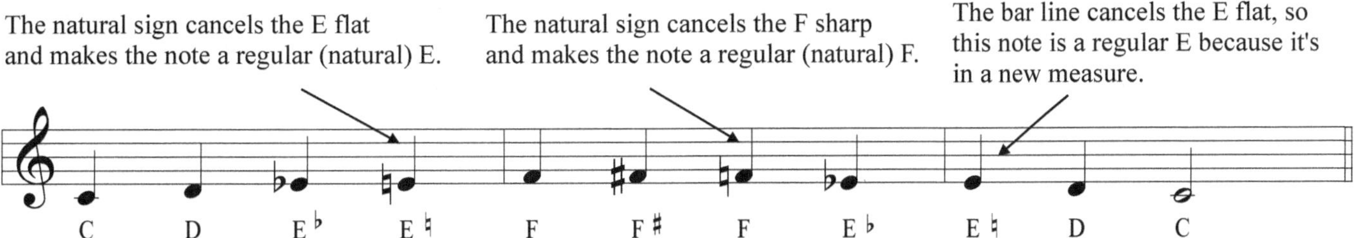

A natural sign also cancels a ♯/♭ that is present in a key signature. Look the example below.

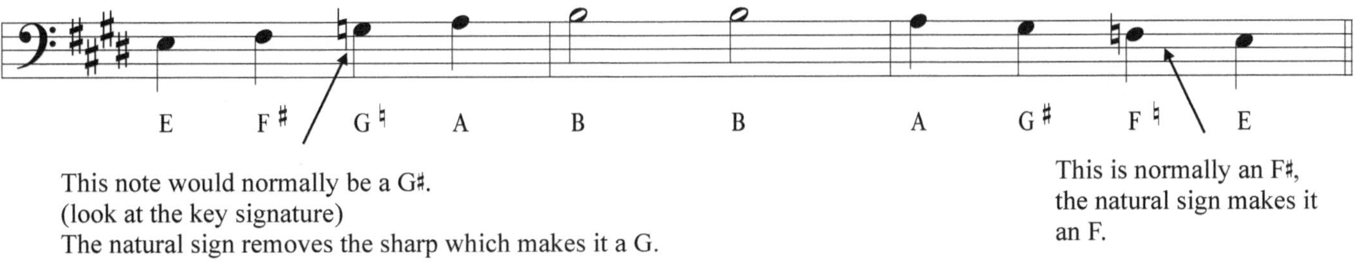

If an accidental (♯/♭) is added to a note and that same note appears in the same measure, it is still flatted/sharped. A natural sign or barline is the only thing that will cancel an added accidental.

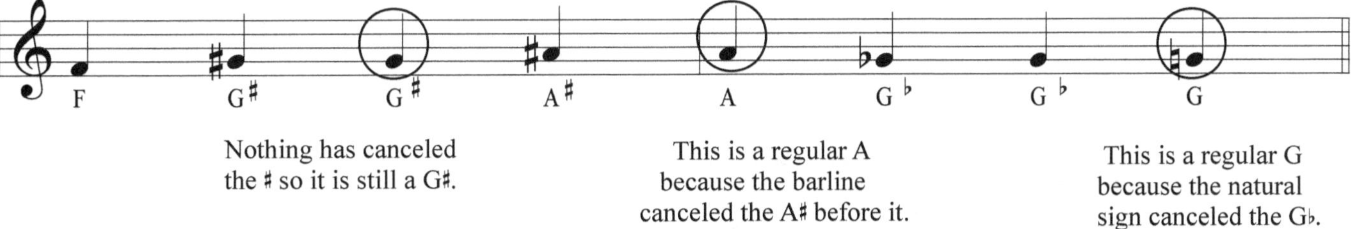

The picture below shows a piano keyboard with the sharps, flats and natural notes.

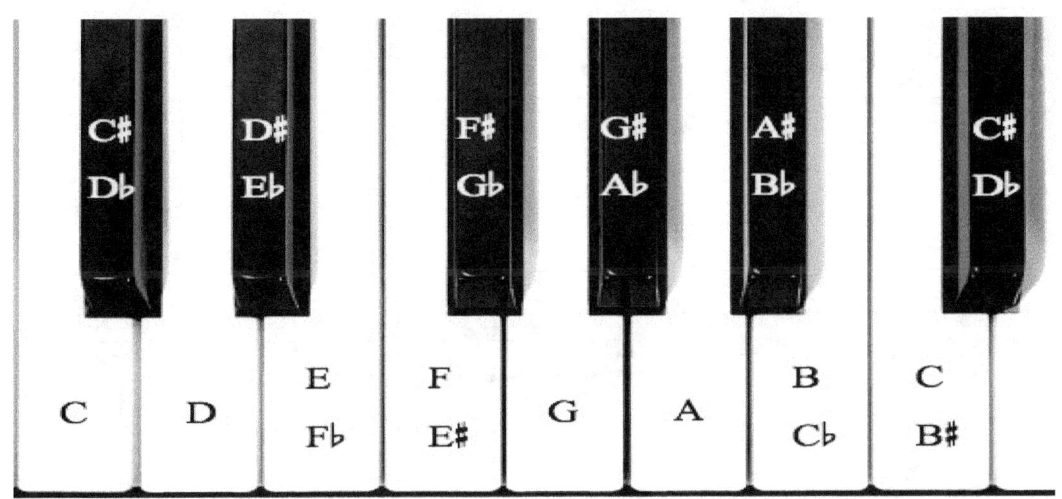

Review: Lesson 1

1. Name the following notes: Pay attention to the clefs & accidentals! The first one is done for you.

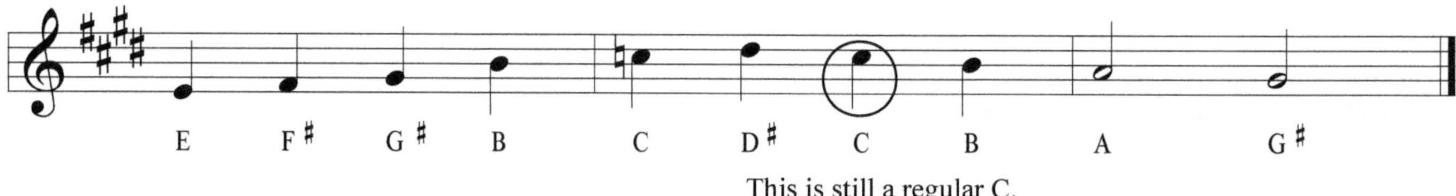

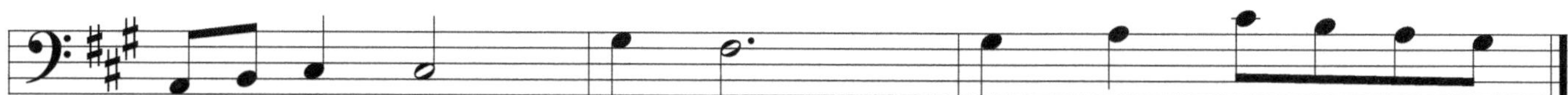

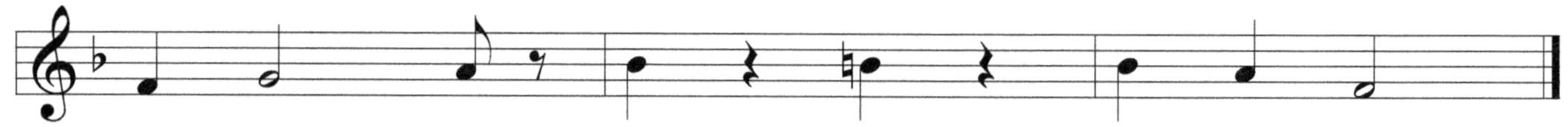

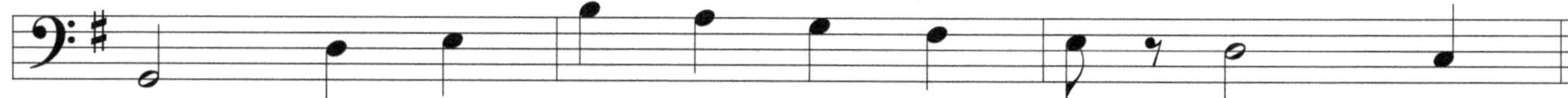

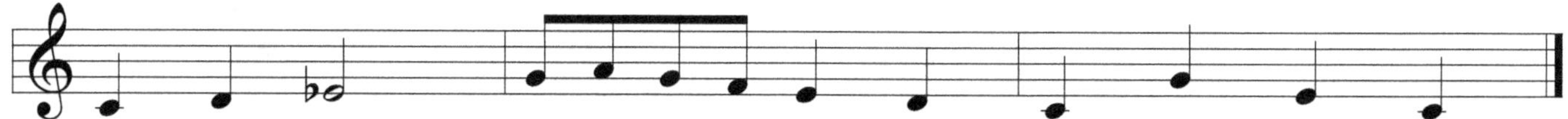

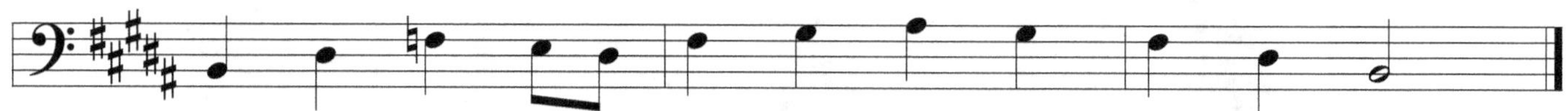

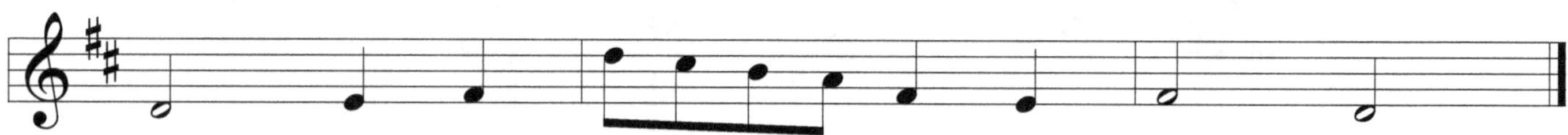

2. Draw a natural sign before each note on the staves below. Make sure the center part of the natural is on the same line or space as the note. The first one is done for you.

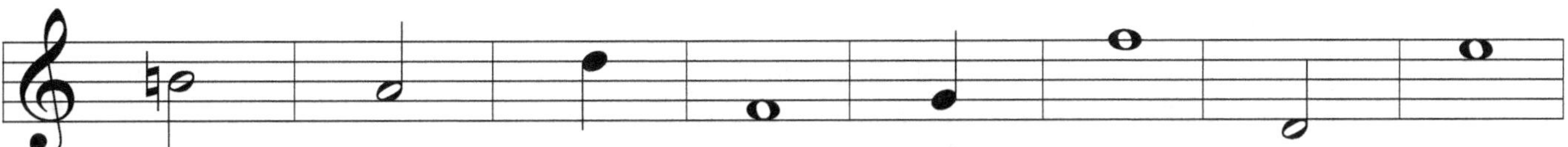

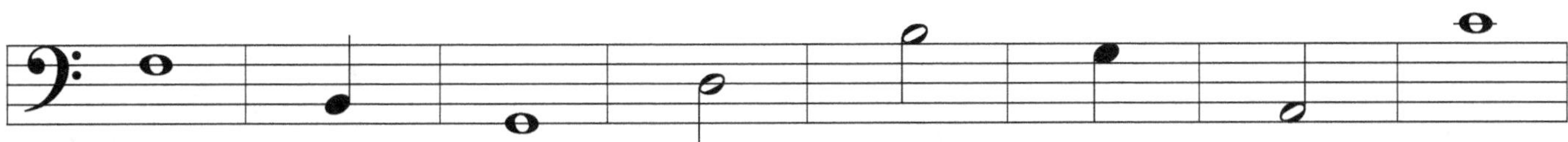

3. Draw a sharp sign before each note on the staves below. Make sure the center part of the sharp is on the same line or space as the note. The first one is done for you.

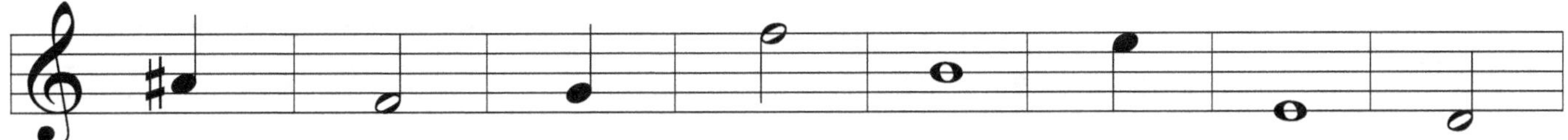

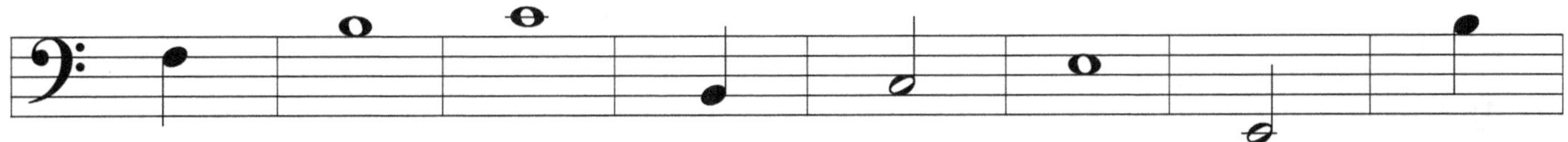

4. Draw a flat sign before each note on the staves below. Make sure the center part of the flat is on the same line or space as the note. The first one is done for you.

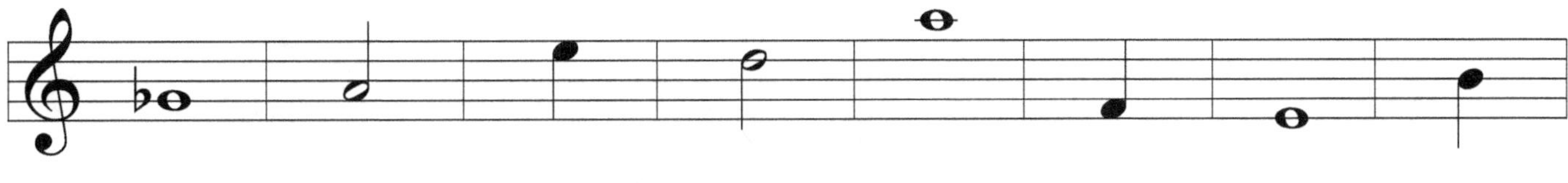

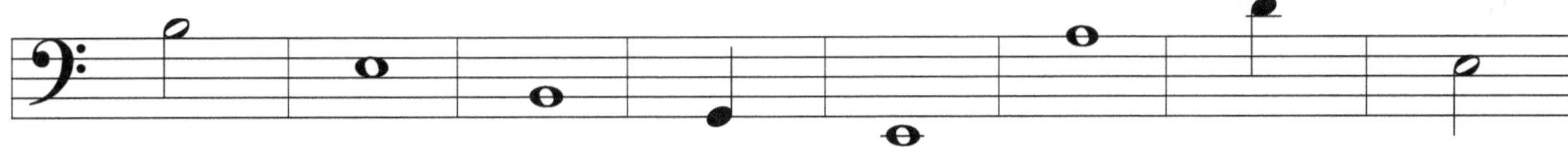

Lesson 2: Note & Rest Values

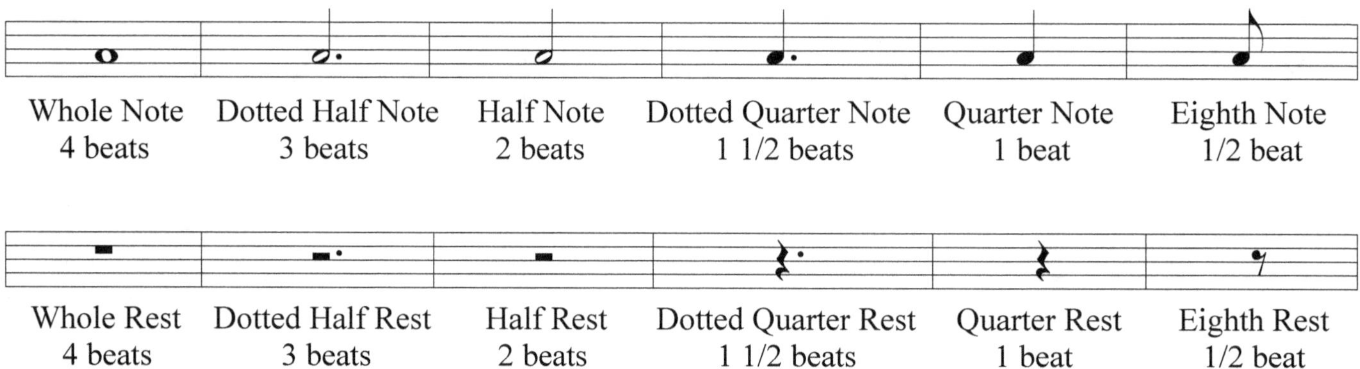

Eighth Notes

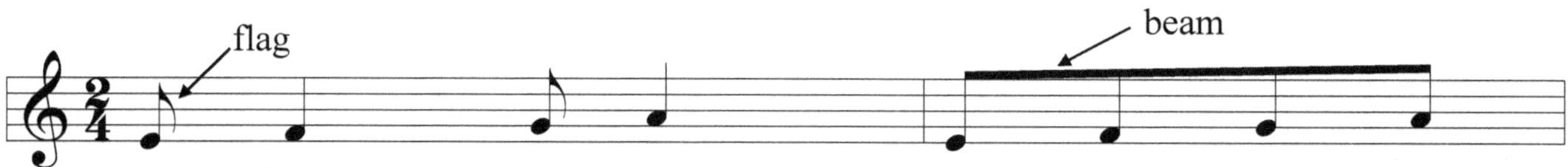

Single eighth notes are written with a flag.

When 2 or more eighth notes are next to each other, they are usually joined by a beam. In music, this is easier to read.

Dotted Quarter Note

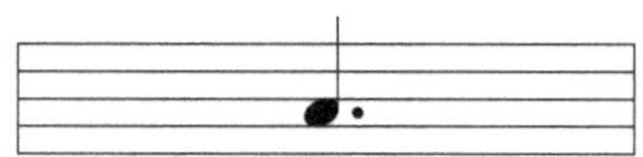

Adding a dot to a note lengthens a note by half of its value. For instance, a quarter note is worth 1 beat, so the dot is worth 1/2 beat. Add the beats together and a dotted quarter note is worth 1 1/2 beats.

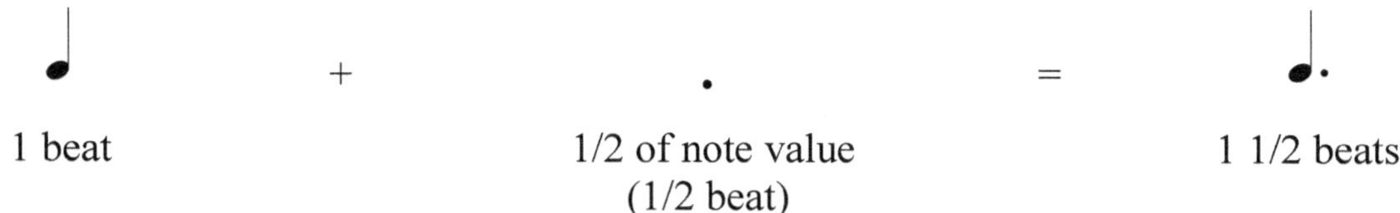

Dotted Quarter Rest

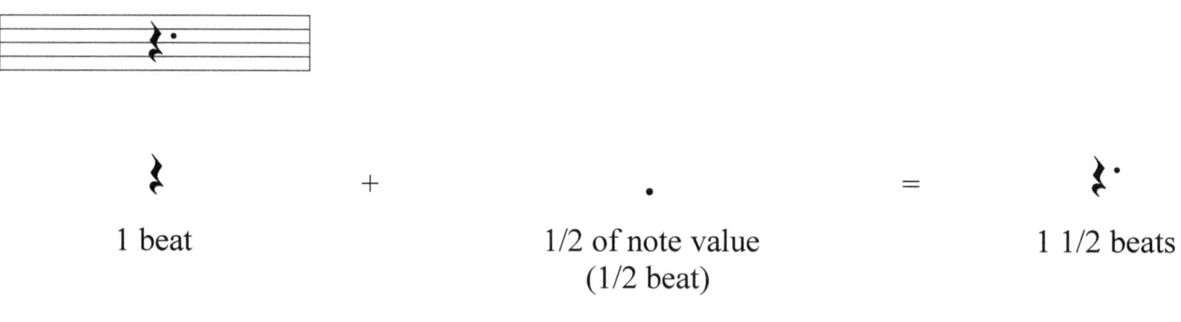

Counting dotted rhythms can be tricky. Dots lengthen a note by 1/2 of it's value, so the following note is usually a short note. Look at the example below...

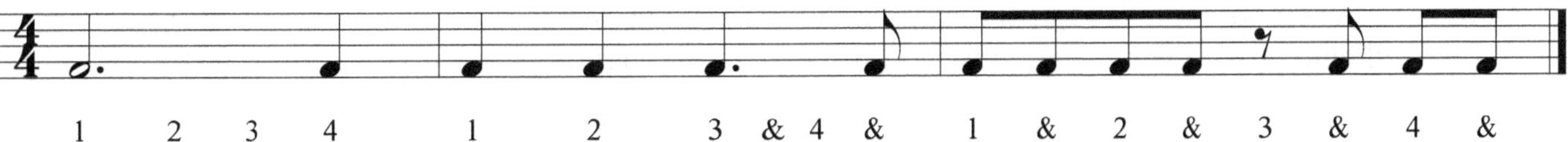

We want to say a count for every note and rest we see. That's why we have 1 & 2 &, etc.

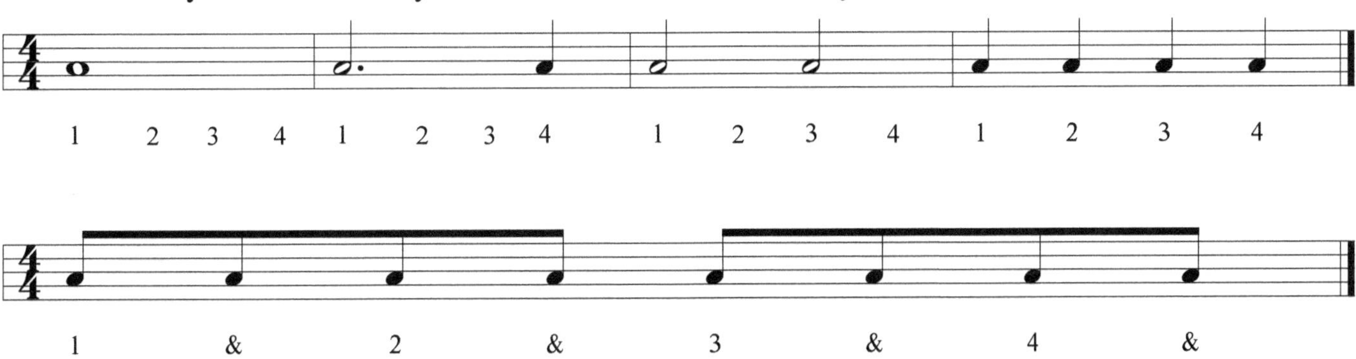

The dotted quarter note is especially difficult because it is worth 1 1/2 beats. Think of three eighth notes fitting into a dotted quarter note. Look at the example below.

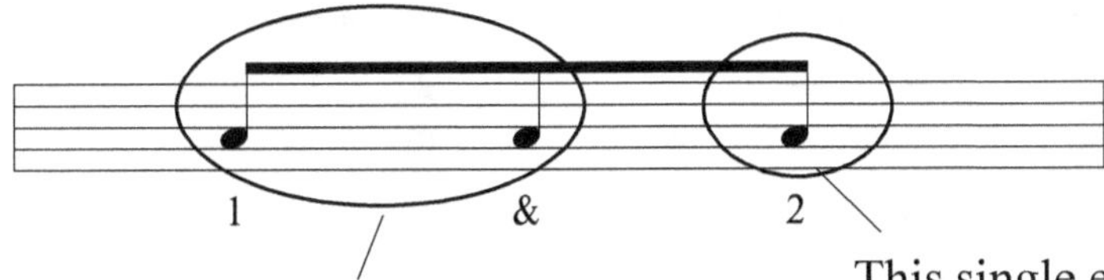

Each eighth note is worth 1/2 beat. These two eighth notes combined equal 1 beat (the same as a quarter note).

This single eighth note is worth 1/2 beat. The dot in a dotted quarter note is also worth 1/2 beat.

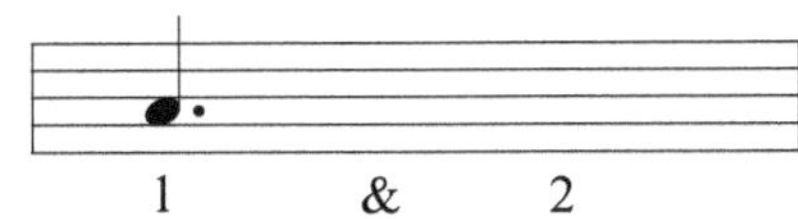

Here are some more examples of how to count eighth and dotted quarter notes.

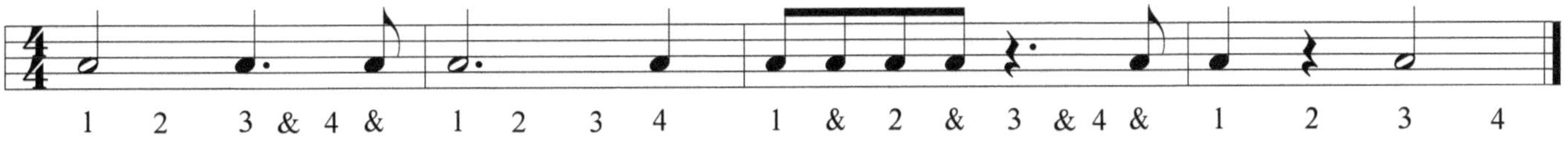

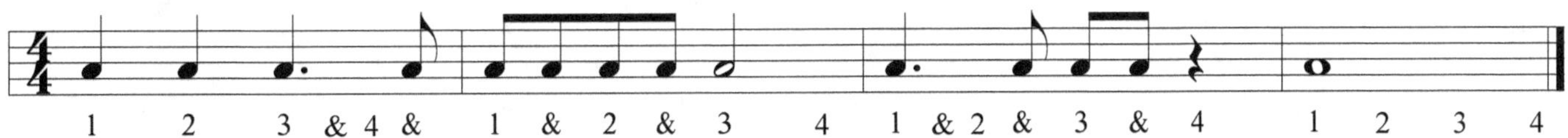

Music Rhythm Tree

Let's take a look at the notes, their values and how they relate with each other. The first example shows how many of each note it takes to fill a measure in 4/4 time (1 whole note, 2 half notes, etc.).
The La's indicate how to sing each note. If you see "La- - -" that means you are holding the note.

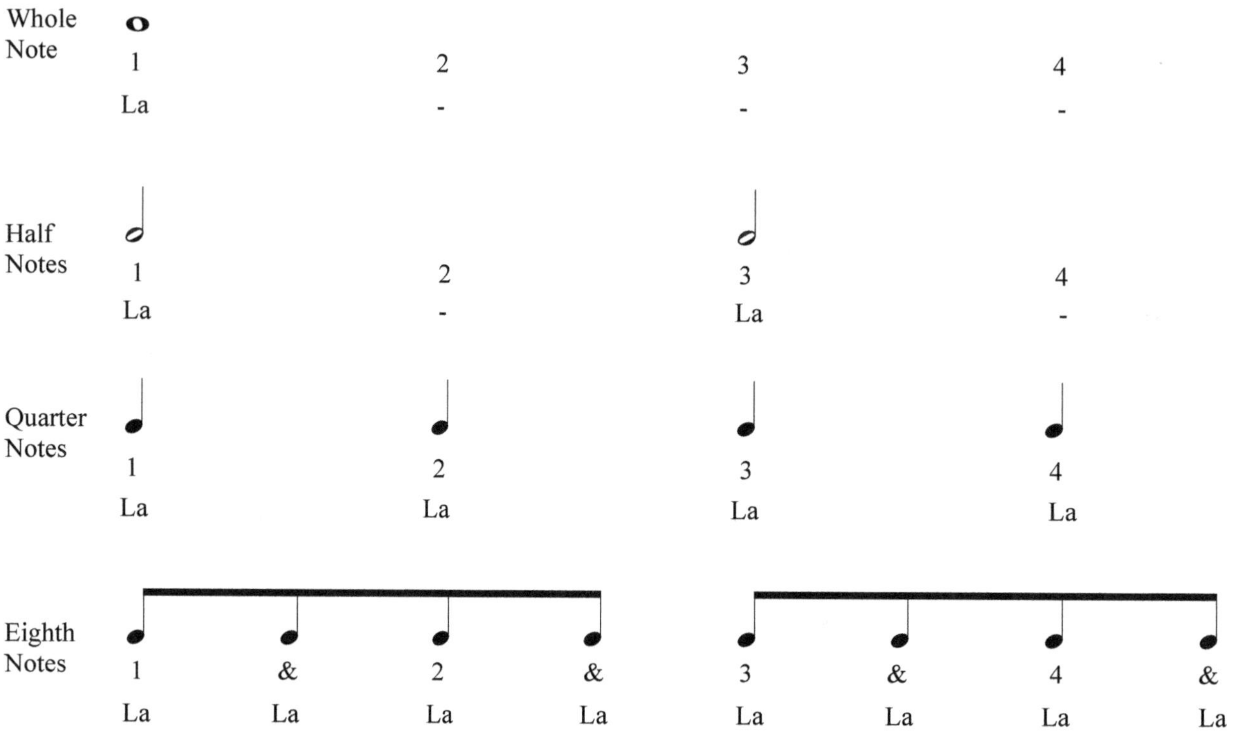

Here's the same music "tree" with rests.

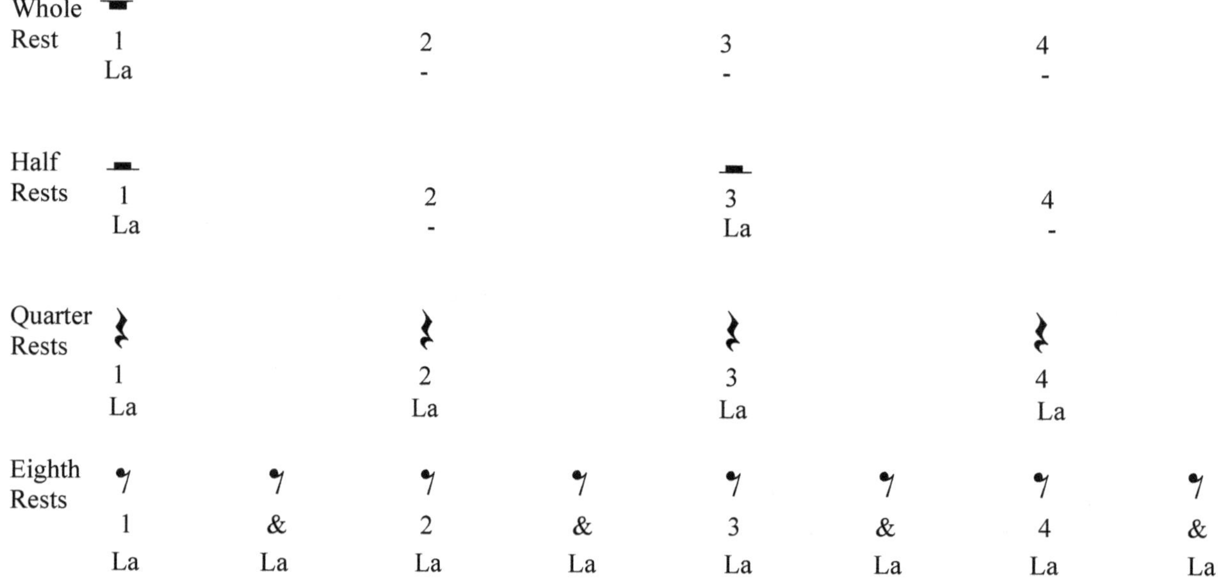

Review: Lesson 2

1. Check the correct counting for each of these examples.

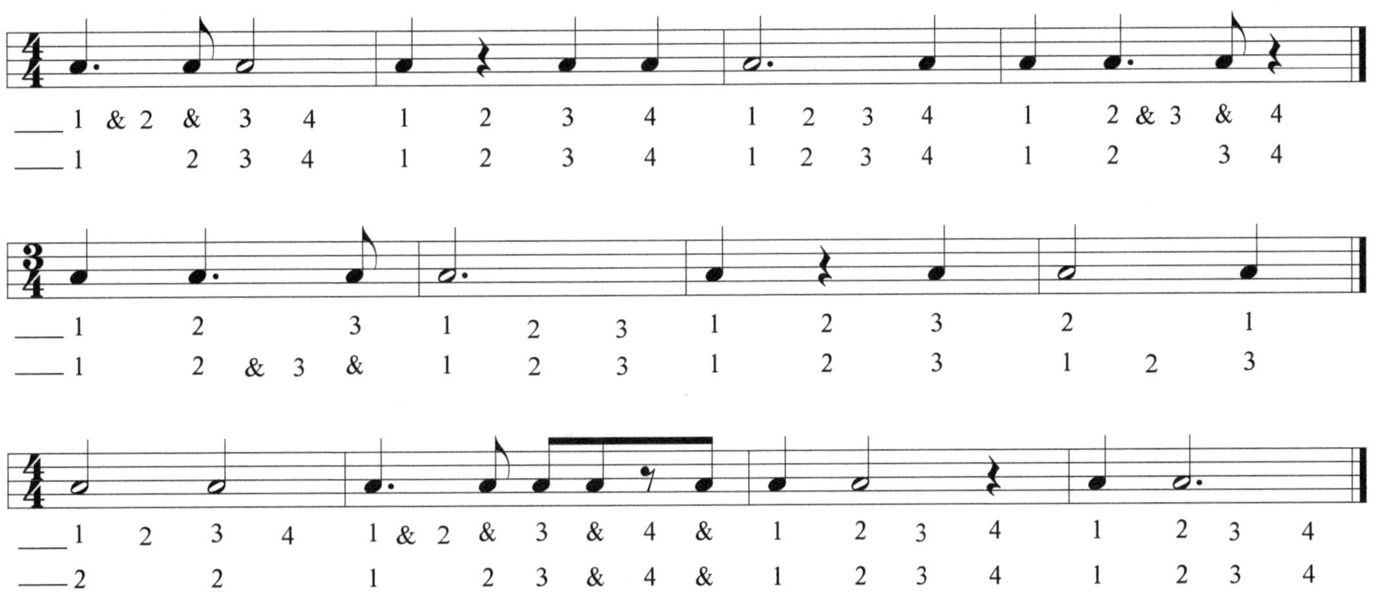

2. Check the correct number of beats each note or rest will receive in $\frac{4}{4}$ time.

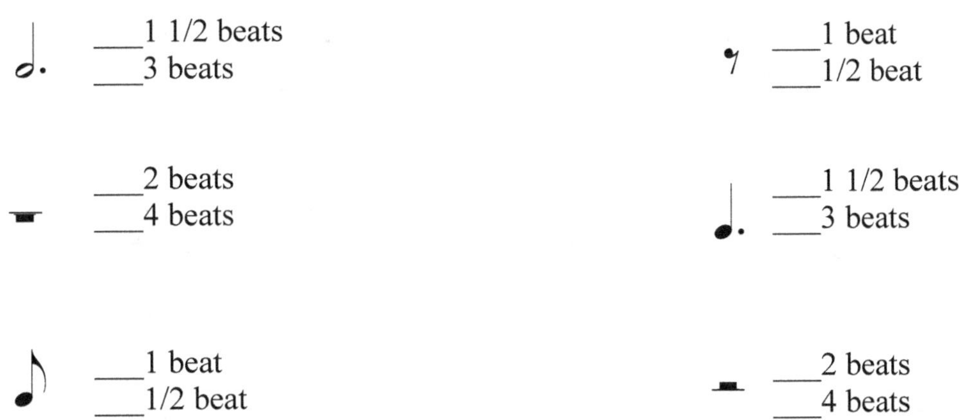

3. Circle the correct name for each note or rest.

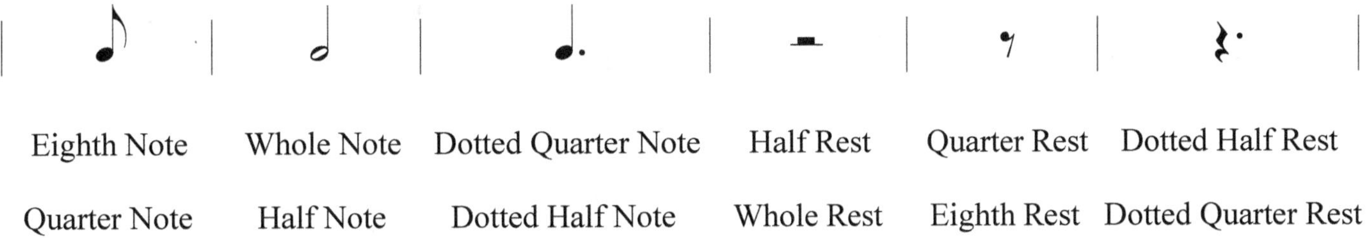

4. Write the beats under the notes, then add missing bar lines and a double bar line to each example.

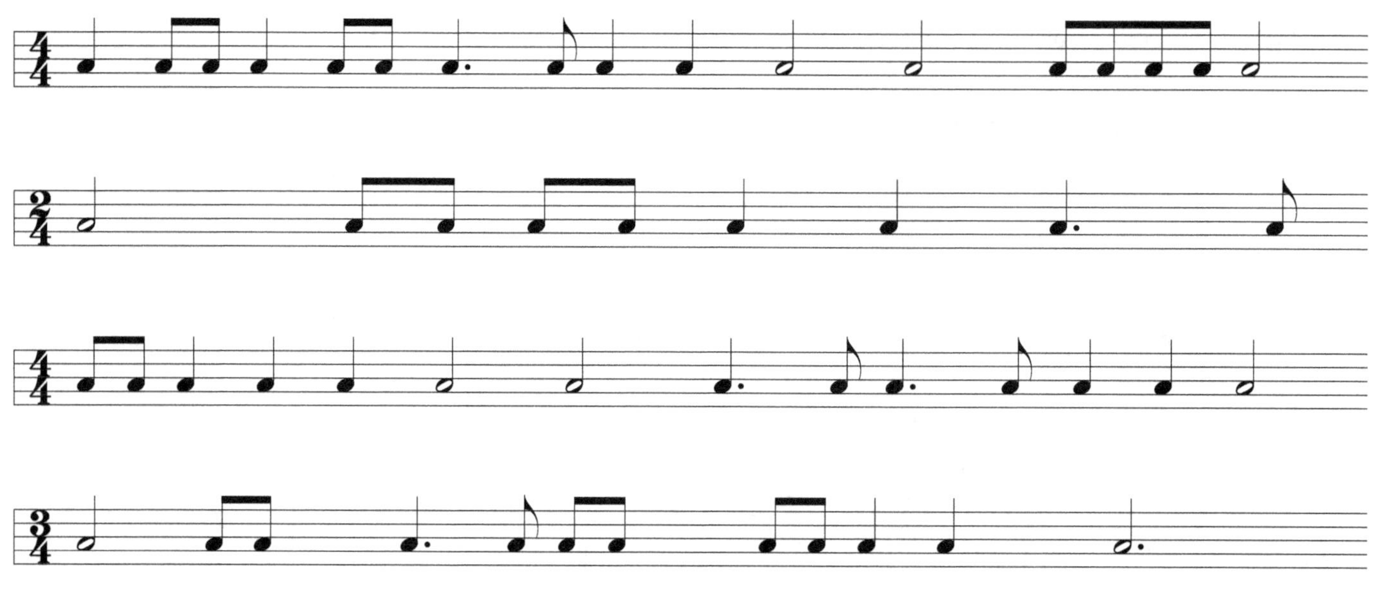

5. Add the missing time signature to the following examples.

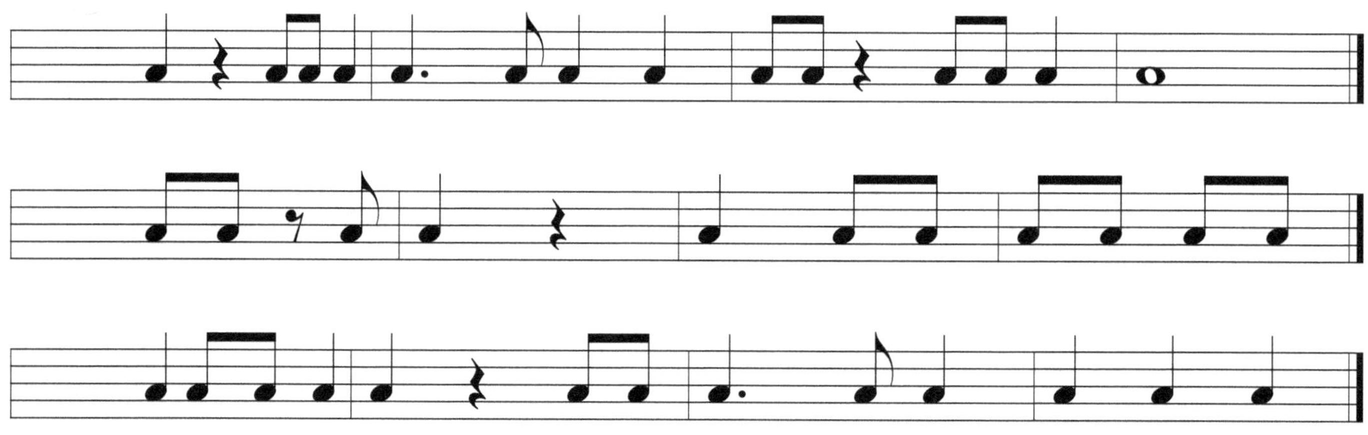

6. Add **one** missing note or rest to each measure.

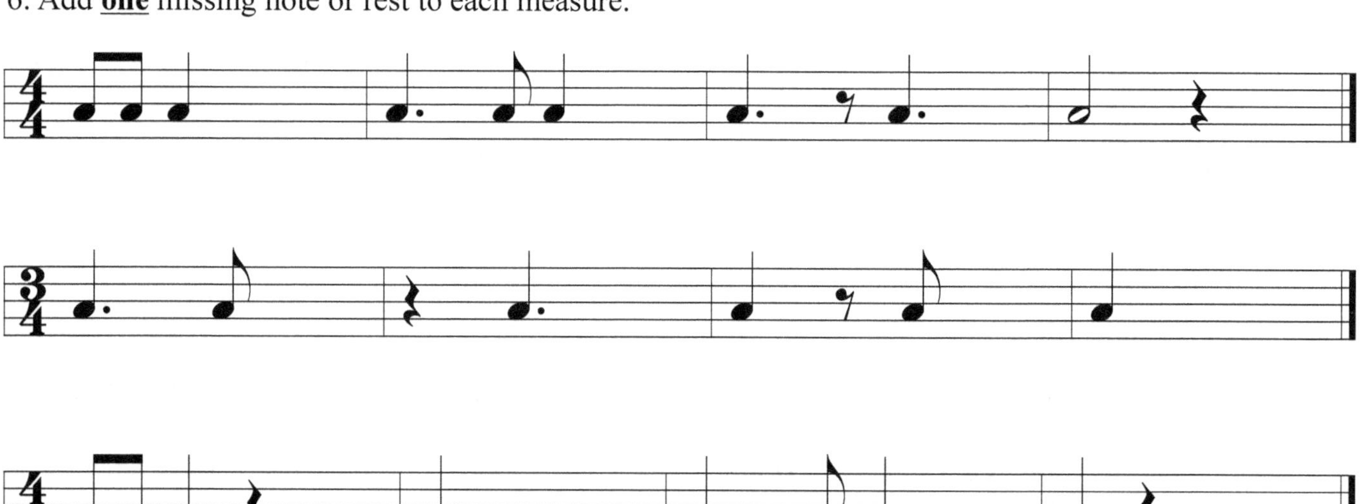

7. Write the beats under the notes/rests in each example, then write La's according to how you would sing the notes. You can use dashes to indicate held notes. Try singing the rhythms on a single pitch once you've written in the La's. The first example is done for you.

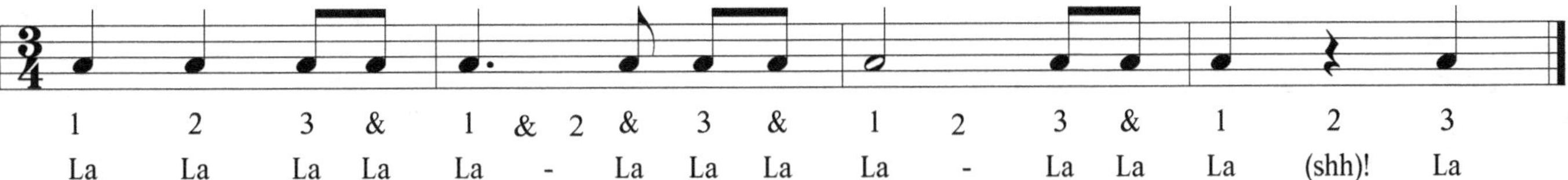

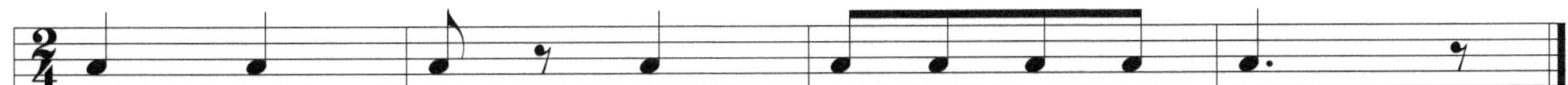

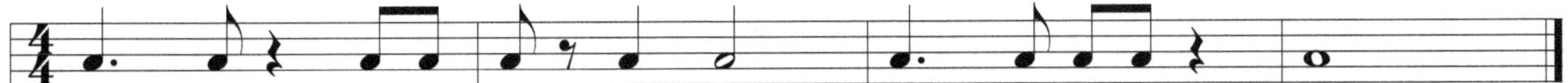

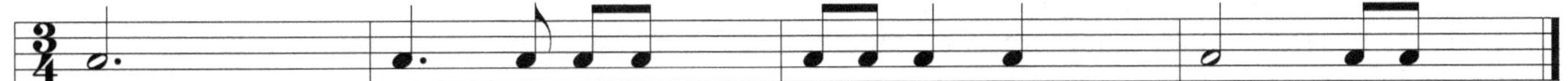

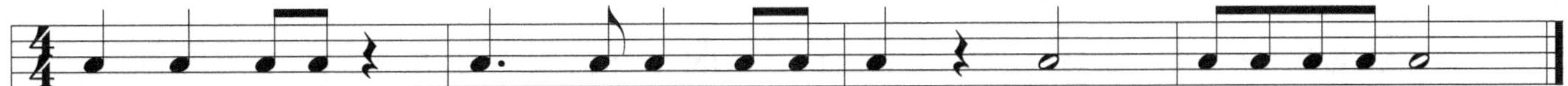

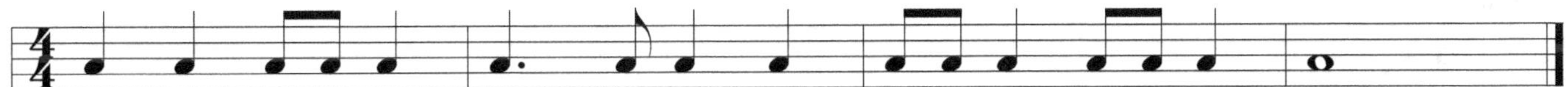

Lesson 3: Notes on the Staff (Review)

Here are the treble clef notes on the staff, including ledger line notes.

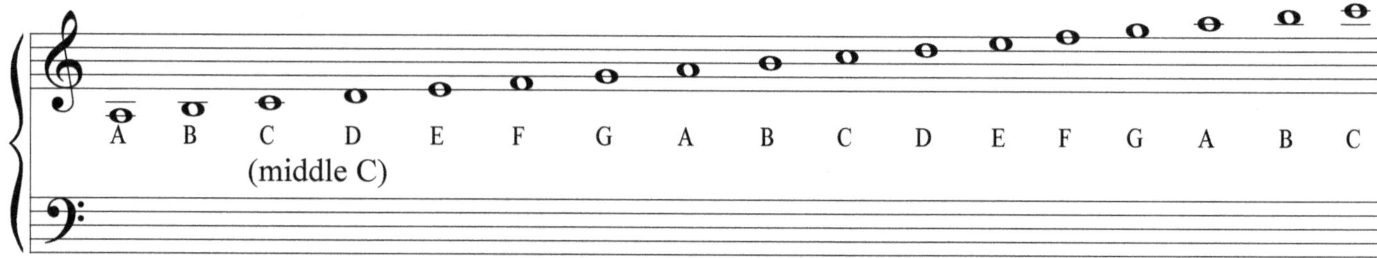

Here are the bass clef notes on the staff, including ledger line notes.

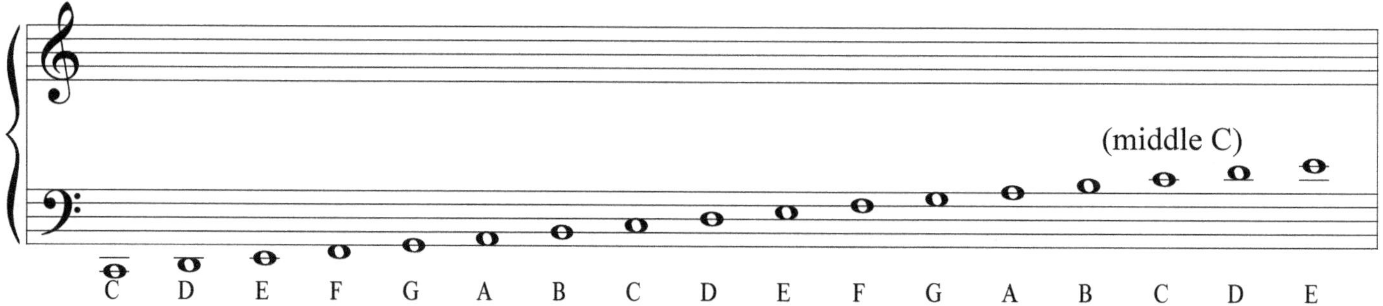

Some key things to remember about notes on the staff:

1. Notes that are stepping alternate between lines and spaces: Line-Space-Line-Space...
2. Ascending notes (notes going up) are in order in the alphabet: A-B-C-D...
3. Descending notes (notes going down) are backwards in the alphabet: D-C-B-A...
4. Ledger lines (short lines that represent imaginary staff lines) must be added to notes above and below the staff.

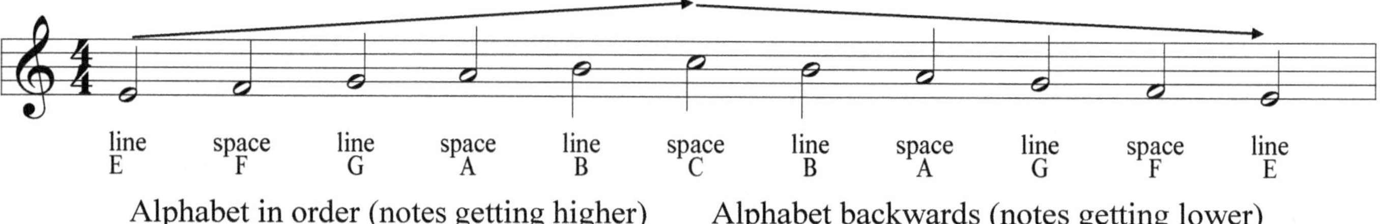

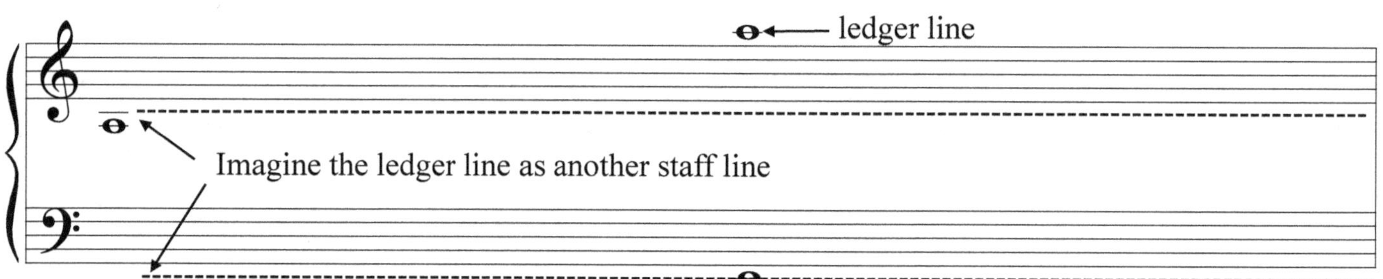

Review: Lesson 3

1. Write the letter name of each note.

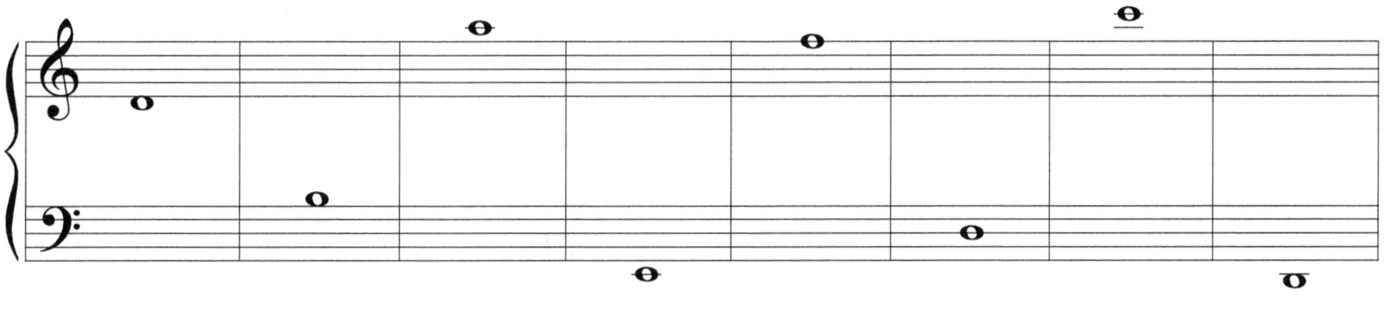

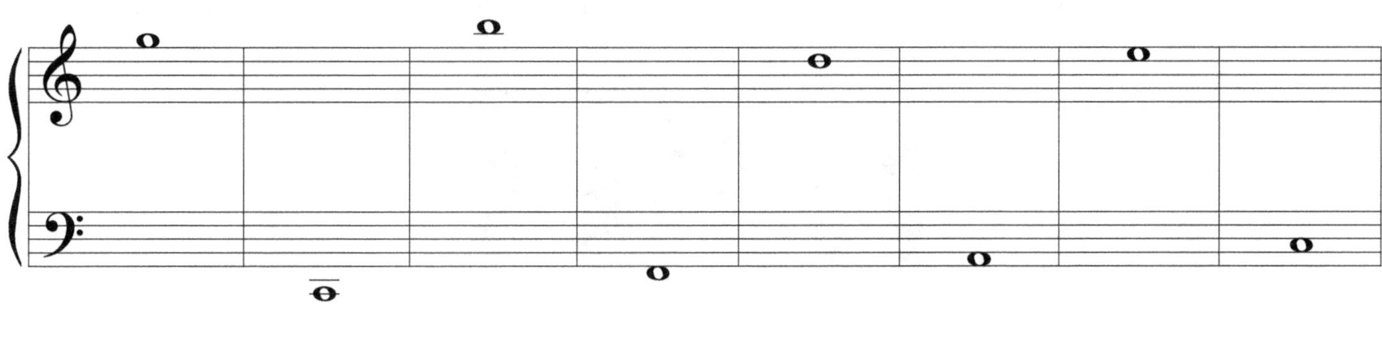

2. Draw the following notes. Use half notes and make sure your stems are going in the right direction.

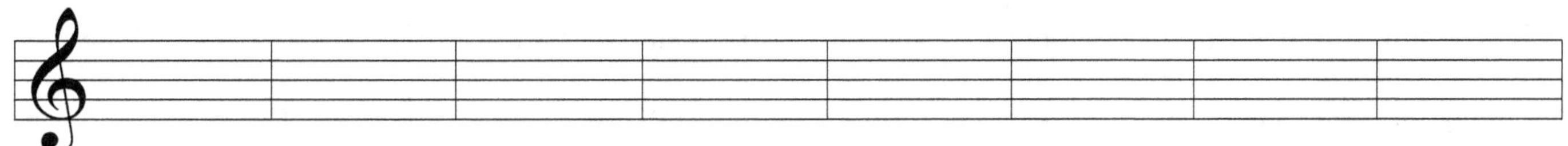

G	A	B	B	C	D	A	middle C
above the staff	below the staff	above the staff	below the staff	above the staff	below the staff	above the staff	ledger line

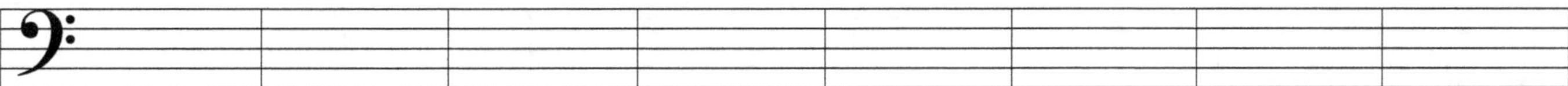

E	D	F	B	C	E	D	middle C
below the staff	above the staff	below the staff	above the staff	below the staff	above the staff	below the staff	ledger line

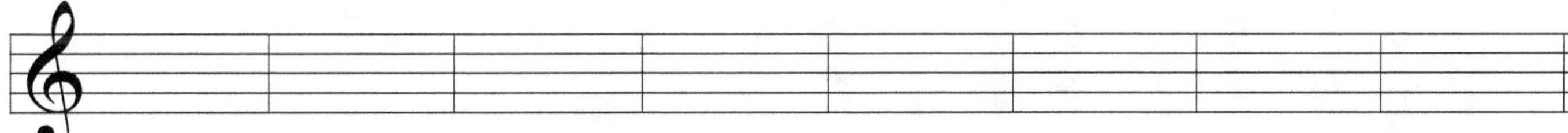

middle C	G	B	C	D	A	A	B
ledger line	above the staff	below the staff	above the staff	below the staff	above the staff	below the staff	above the staff

Lesson 4: Key Signatures

In music, a Key Signature is a series of sharp (♯) or flat (♭) symbols placed on the staff immediately after the Treble and Bass clefs. The Key Signature also creates the tonal center for a piece.

The key signature shows which notes are to be sung a half step higher (sharp) or a half step lower (flat) for the duration of the piece.

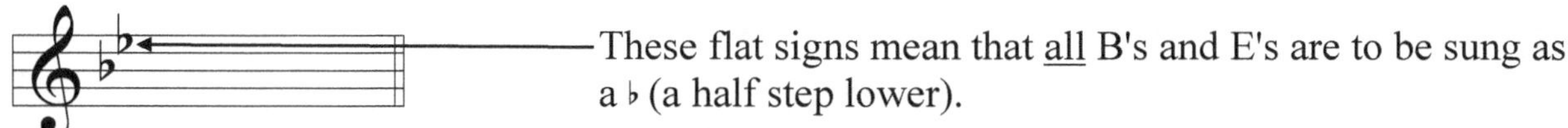

These flat signs mean that all B's and E's are to be sung as a ♭ (a half step lower).

A half step is the distance from one pitch to the very next pitch (up or down), while a whole step is comprised of 2 half steps (up or down). This is easy to see on a piano keyboard like the one below.

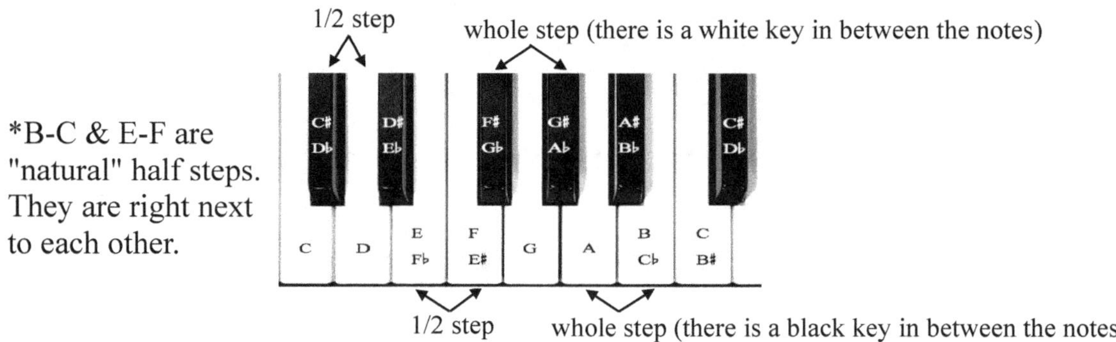

*B-C & E-F are "natural" half steps. They are right next to each other.

The key signature of B♭ Major has a B♭ and E♭ because in order for it to sound Major (or happy), the notes must follow a specific pattern of half steps and whole steps.

The pattern of half steps and whole steps that make up a Major scale (8 notes) is as follows:

Whole - Whole - Half - Whole - Whole - Whole - Half (W - W - H - W - W - W - H)

Take a look at a B♭ Major scale on the staff below. The B♭ & E♭ must be added in order for the formula (pattern of half steps and whole steps) to be correct.

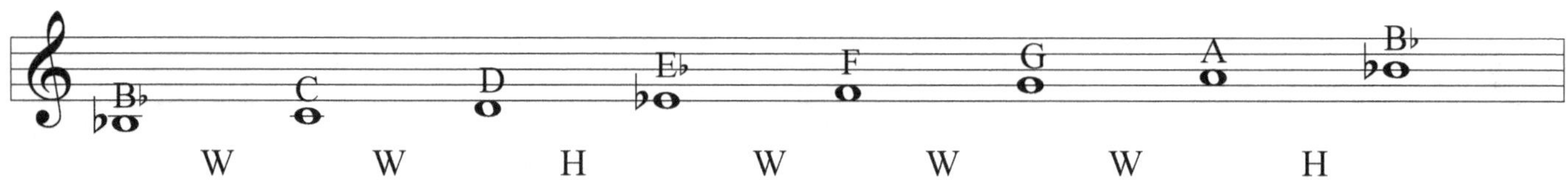

W W H W W W H

Here is what a B♭ Major scale looks like on a piano keyboard.

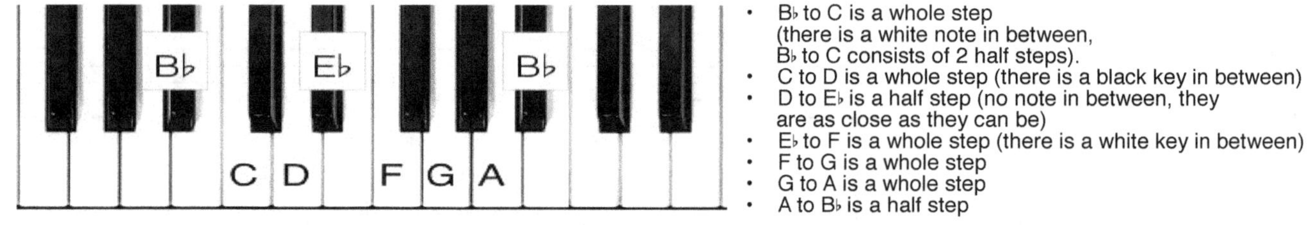

- B♭ to C is a whole step (there is a white note in between, B♭ to C consists of 2 half steps).
- C to D is a whole step (there is a black key in between)
- D to E♭ is a half step (no note in between, they are as close as they can be)
- E♭ to F is a whole step (there is a white key in between)
- F to G is a whole step
- G to A is a whole step
- A to B♭ is a half step

*Remember the "natural half steps" between B-C and E-F. These pitches are right next to each other. Look at the keyboard above to see how close they are on a piano!

In this Level, we are going to study 3 new key signatures: B♭ Major, E♭ Major & A♭ Major. You learned C, G, F and D Major in Level 1, and A, E and B Major in Level 2.

Look at the Major scales below for these key signatures so you can see how the Major scale pattern, W-W-H-W-W-W-H includes the necessary accidentals (sharps/flats).

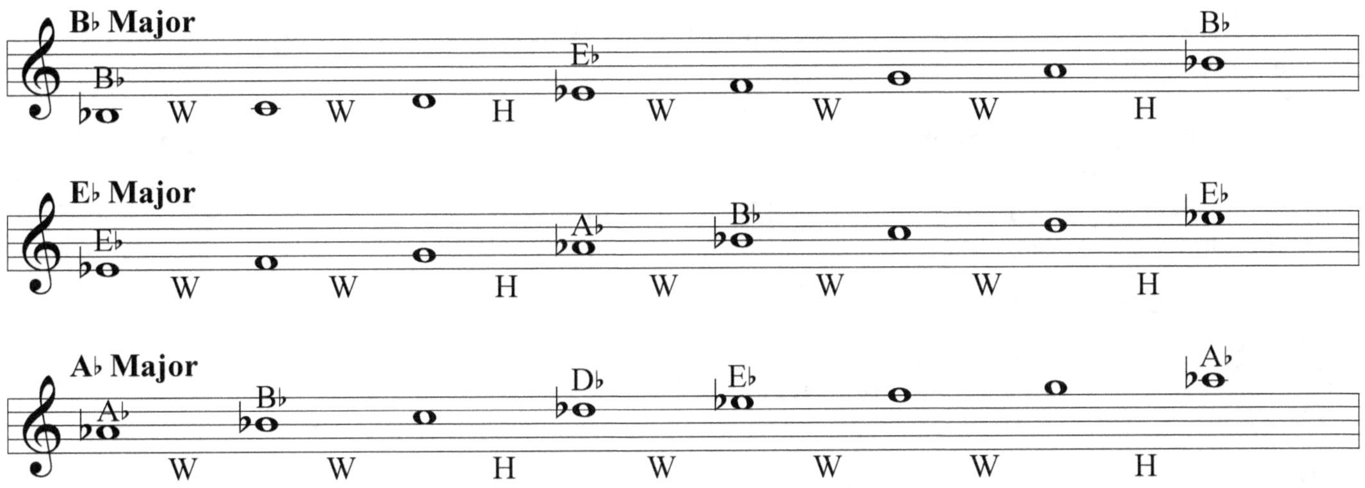

Here are the key signatures for the scales.

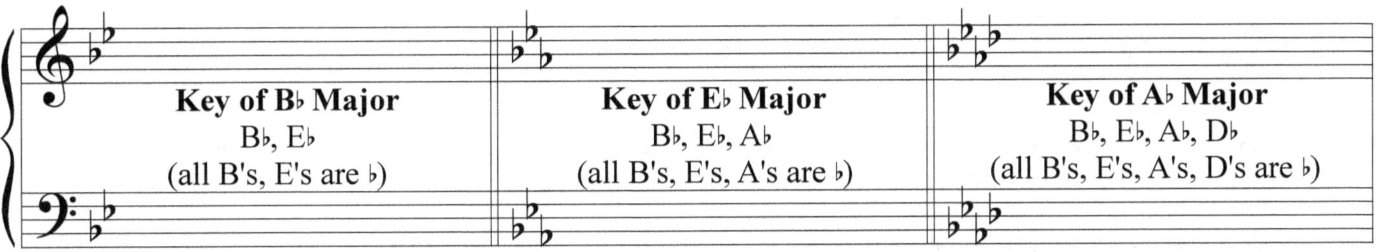

Here is what the scales look like with a key signature. The flatted notes are circled.

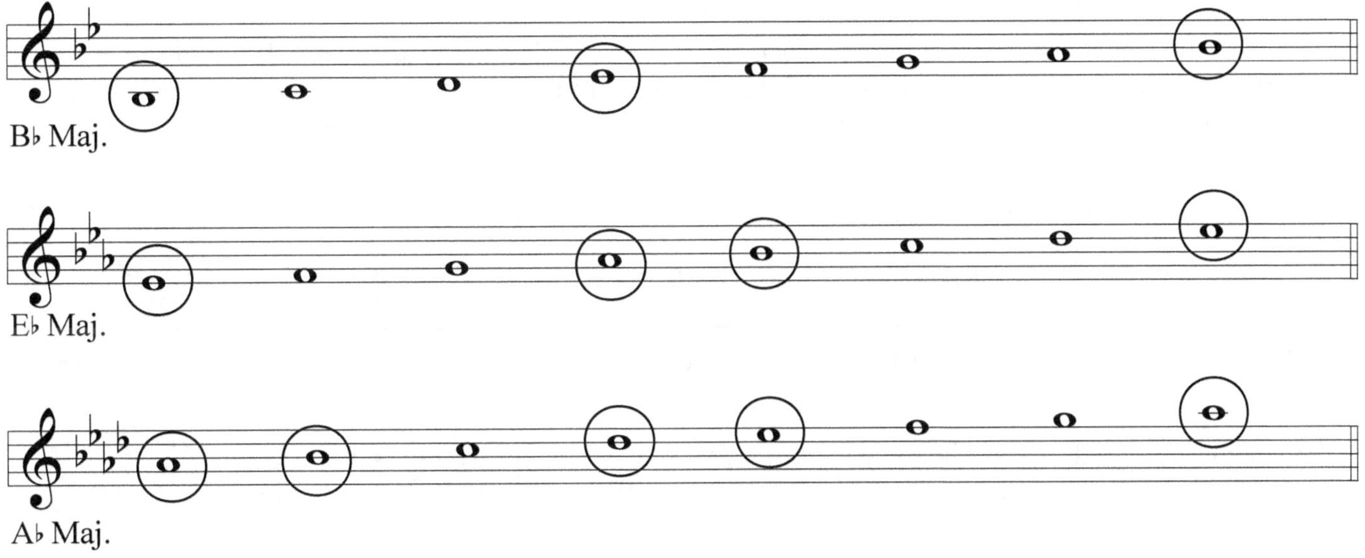

If you don't remember the formula for the Major scale, here are some additional tools for remembering how to identify a key signature.

For flat keys (key signatures with flats), there are two easy ways to identify a key signature.

1. Look at the second to the last flat, and that's the key!
   In E♭ Major, for example, there are three flats; B♭, E♭, & A♭. The second to the last flat is E♭, and that's the key.

2. Look at the last flat (farthest to the right), and it is the "Fa" in the Major scale. If the last flat (farthest to the right) is "Fa" then count up 4 more notes to find "Do." In the key of E♭ Major, A♭ is the last flat in the key signature, so it is "Fa." If A♭ is "Fa" then B♭ is "Sol," C is "La," D is "Ti" and E♭ is "Do." The key is E♭ Major.

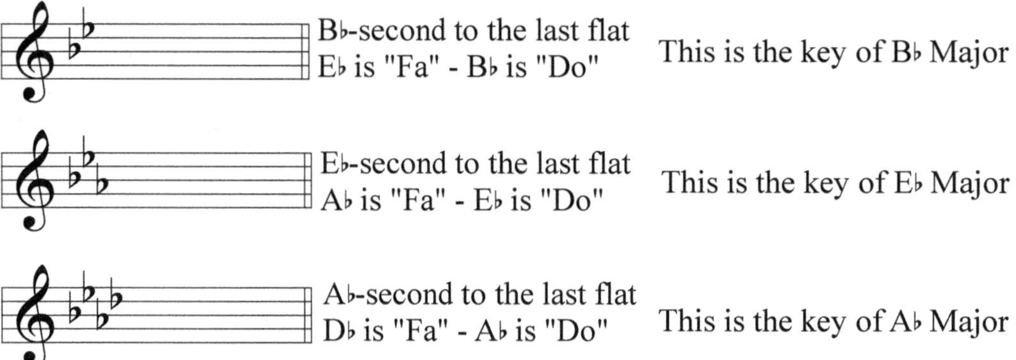

In Levels 1 & 2, you were introduced to the keys of C, F, G, D, A, E & B Major. C has no ♯/♭, F has 1♭ (B♭) and the other keys have sharps in their key signatures.

For sharp keys (key signatures with sharps), there are two easy ways to identify a key signature.

1. Look at the last sharp (farthest one to the right), then name the next note in the musical alphabet. That's the key! In A Major, for example, the farthest sharp to the right is G♯. The next letter in the musical alphabet is A, so the key is A Major.

2. Look at the last sharp (farthest to the right), and it is the "Ti" in the Major scale. If the last sharp (farthest to the right) is "Ti" then "Do" is the next note. In the key of E Major, D♯ is the last sharp in the key signature, so it is "Ti." If D♯ is "Ti" then E is "Do." The key is E Major.

Here are the key signatures we learned in Levels 1 & 2:

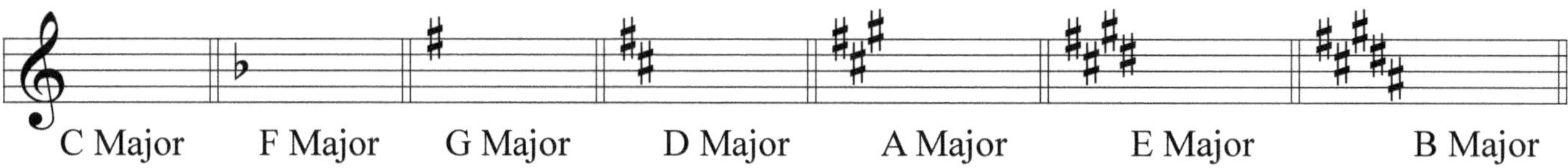

*When sharps or flats appear in a key signature, <u>all</u> sharped or flatted notes are affected; they do not have to be on the same line or space that the sharp and flat are on in the key signature.

Review: Lesson 4

1. Circle the correct pattern of Whole steps and Half steps that create a Major scale.

   a. W H W W W H W

   b. W W H W W W H

2. Add the necessary ♯ or ♭ to the scales below to create Major scales. Make sure you draw the ♯/♭ before the note that is affected. The center part of the sharp and flat must be on the same line/space of the note it is affecting.

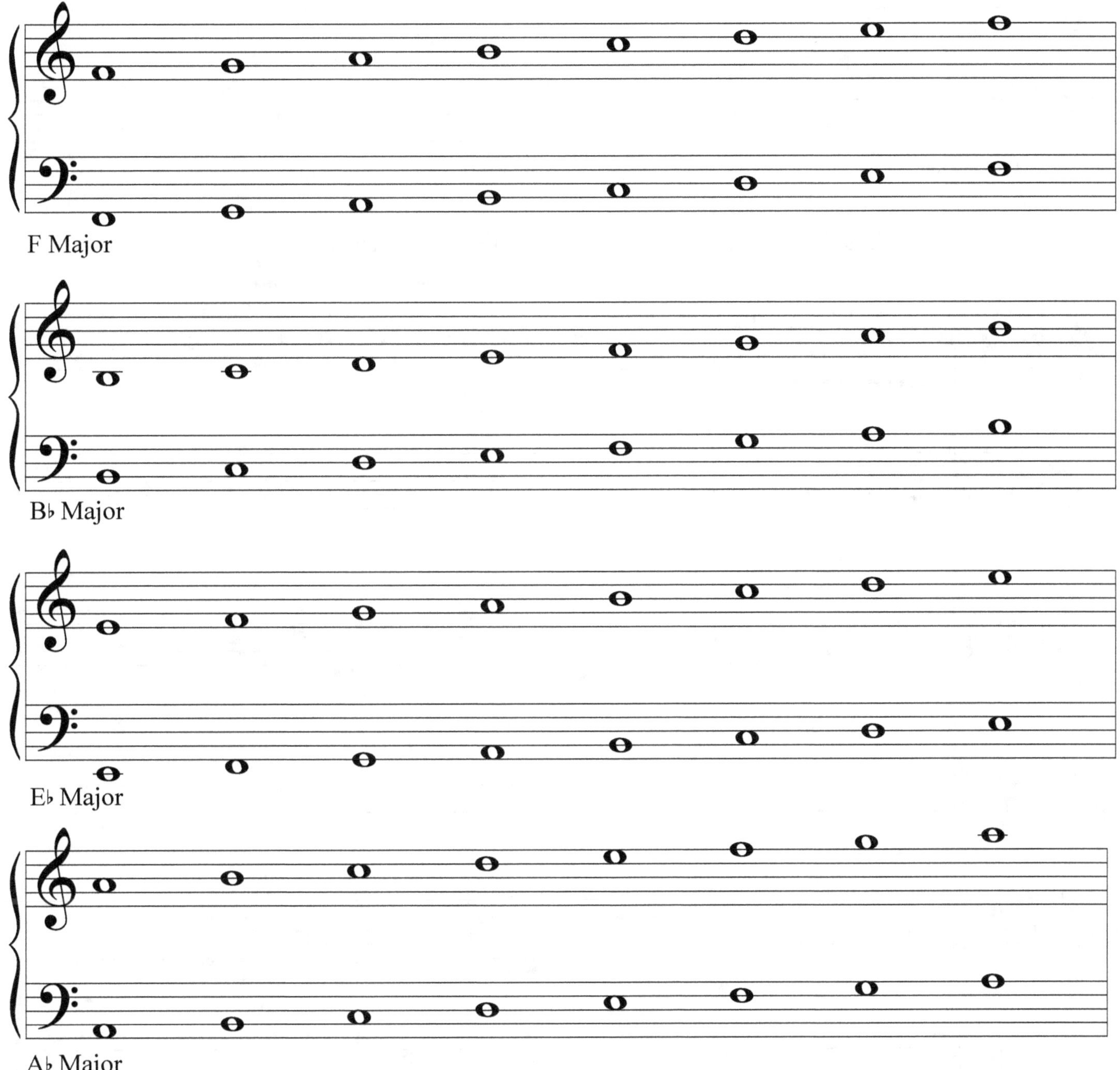

3. Name the Major key for each of these key signatures. The first one is done for you.

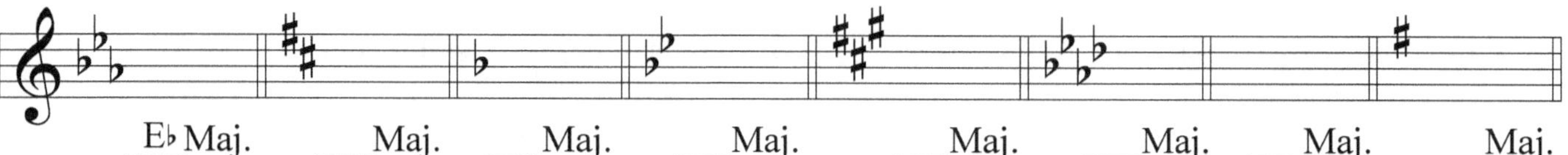

4. Draw the key signature in both the Treble and Bass staves for each of the requested keys. Make sure you add the ♯/♭ to the correct line/space and keep the center part of the ♯/♭ on the correct line/space. Look at question 3 for hints.

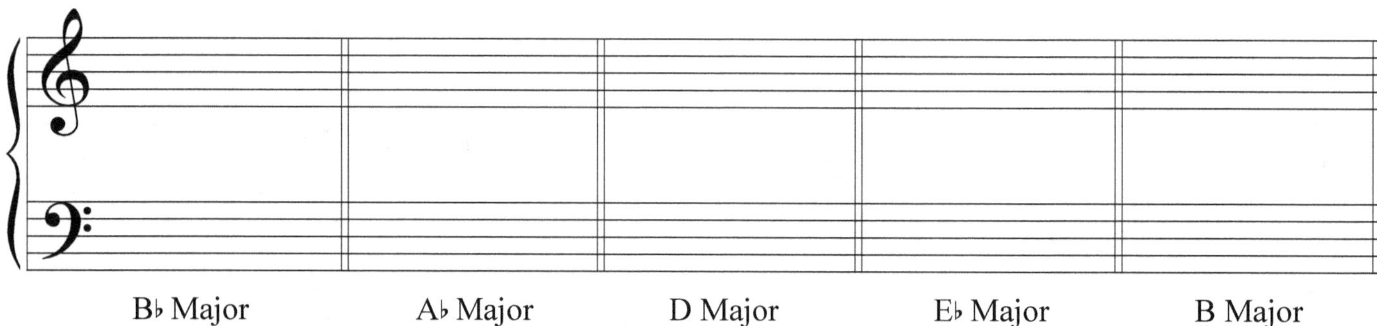

5. Circle the notes affected the by key signature. Pay attention to clef changes.

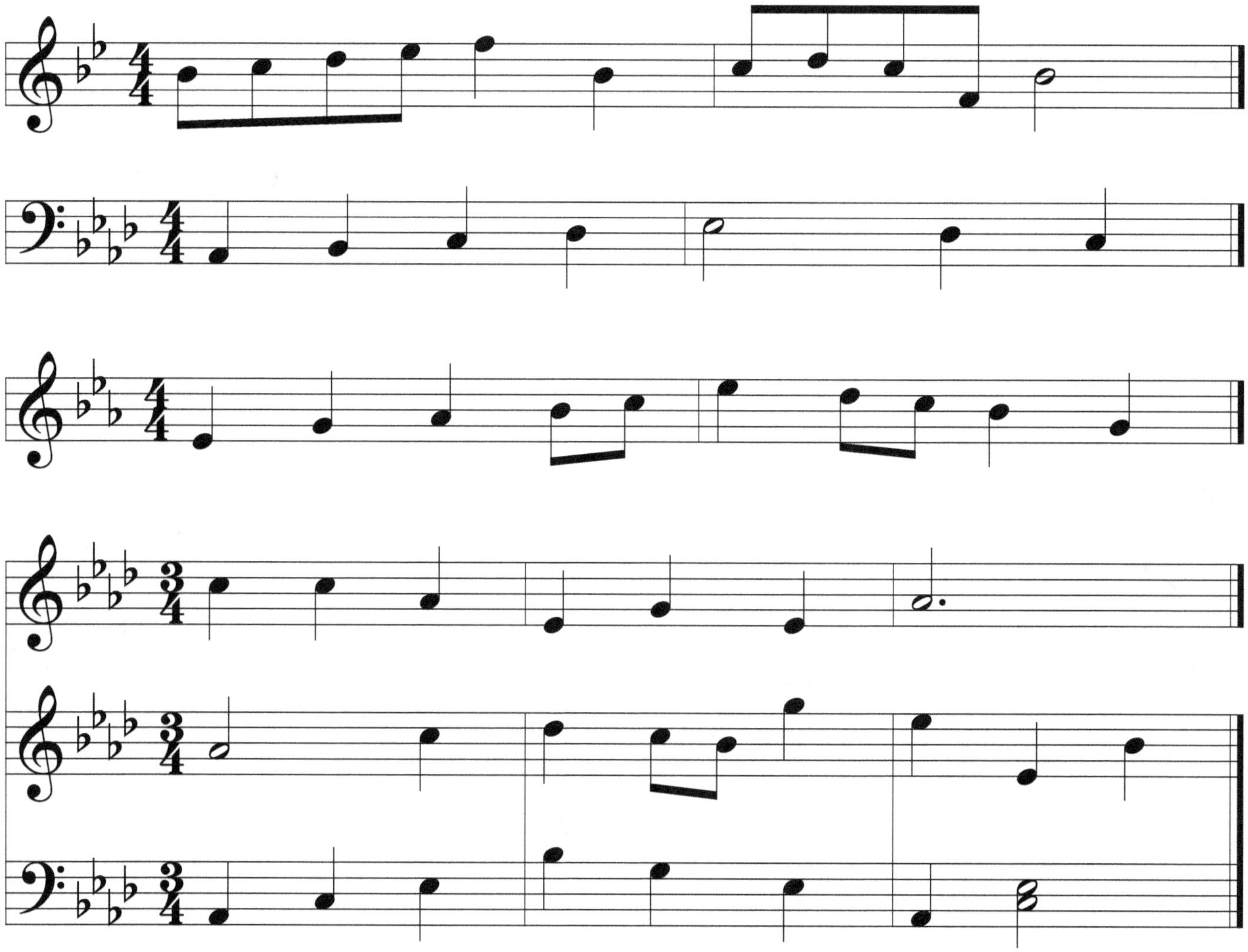

Lesson 5: Triads

A Triad, or 3-note chord, is formed when the first, third and fifth notes of a scale are sung or played, either consecutively or at the same time. The root, or the lowest note of a triad, determines its letter name.

Example B♭ Major. B♭ is the 1st/root, D is the 3rd/middle note, F is the 5th/top note

This is a "root position" chord

The following examples show the Major Scales and Major Triads formed on the first note of the scale (Do). The 1st, 3rd, & 5th notes (Do-Mi-Sol) are circled.

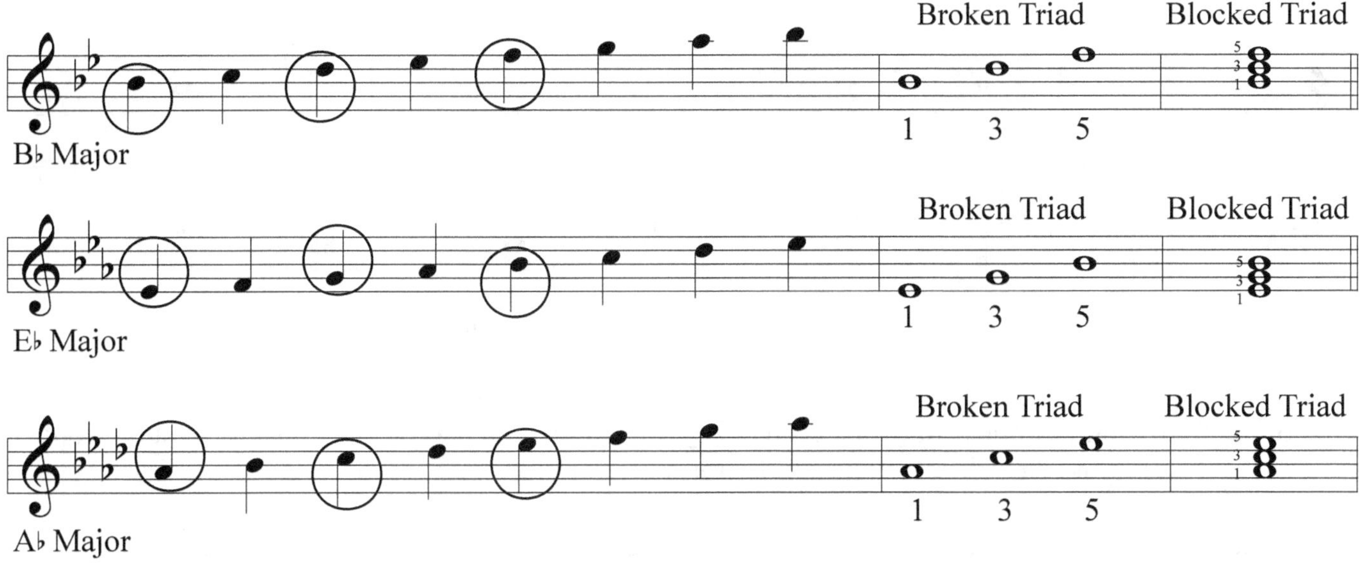

Here are the root position triads in both clefs.

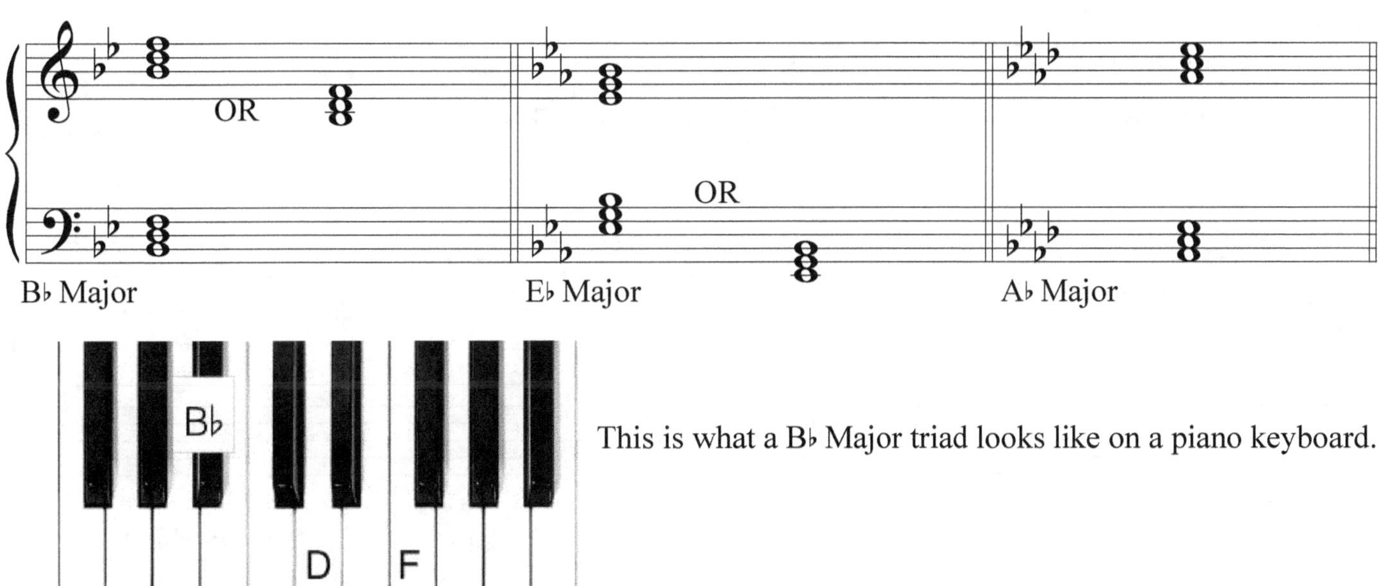

This is what a B♭ Major triad looks like on a piano keyboard.

Review: Lesson 5

1. Name the following triads. Remember, look at the bottom note (root) for the "name" of the triad.

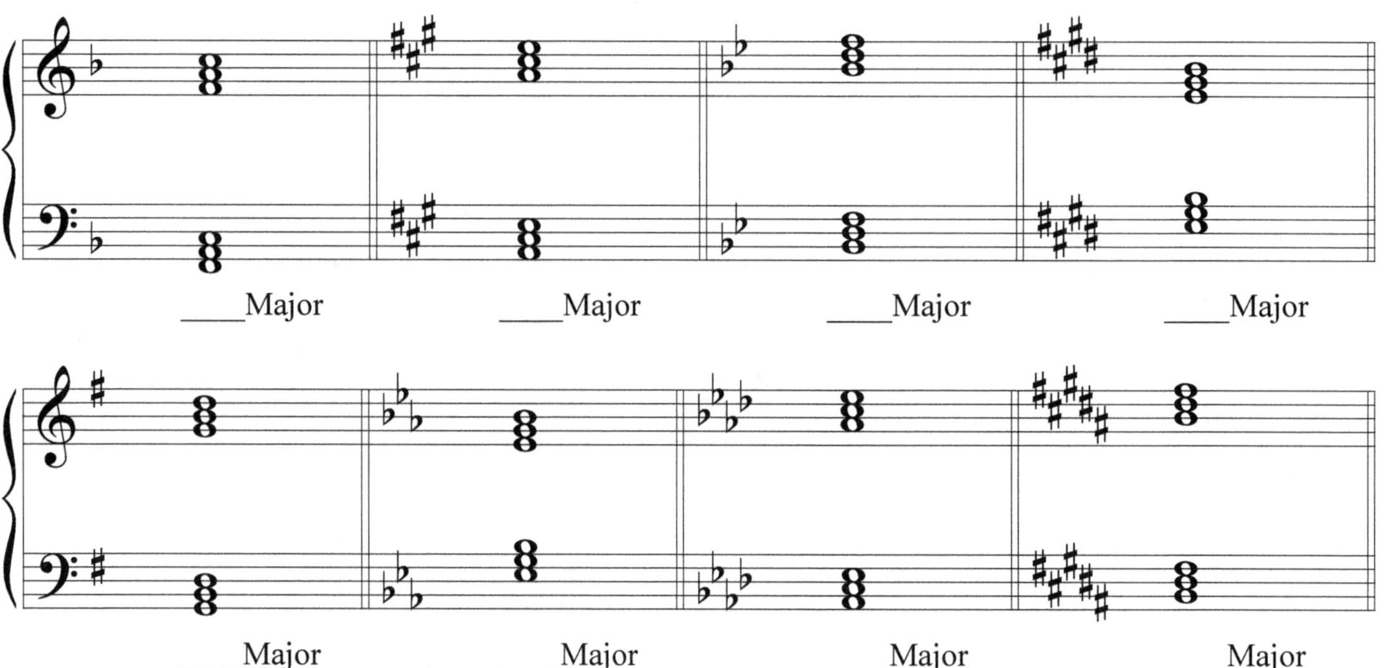

2. For the following examples, draw the correct key signature, then add the root position triads to both the Treble and Bass clefs. Look at question 1 for hints.

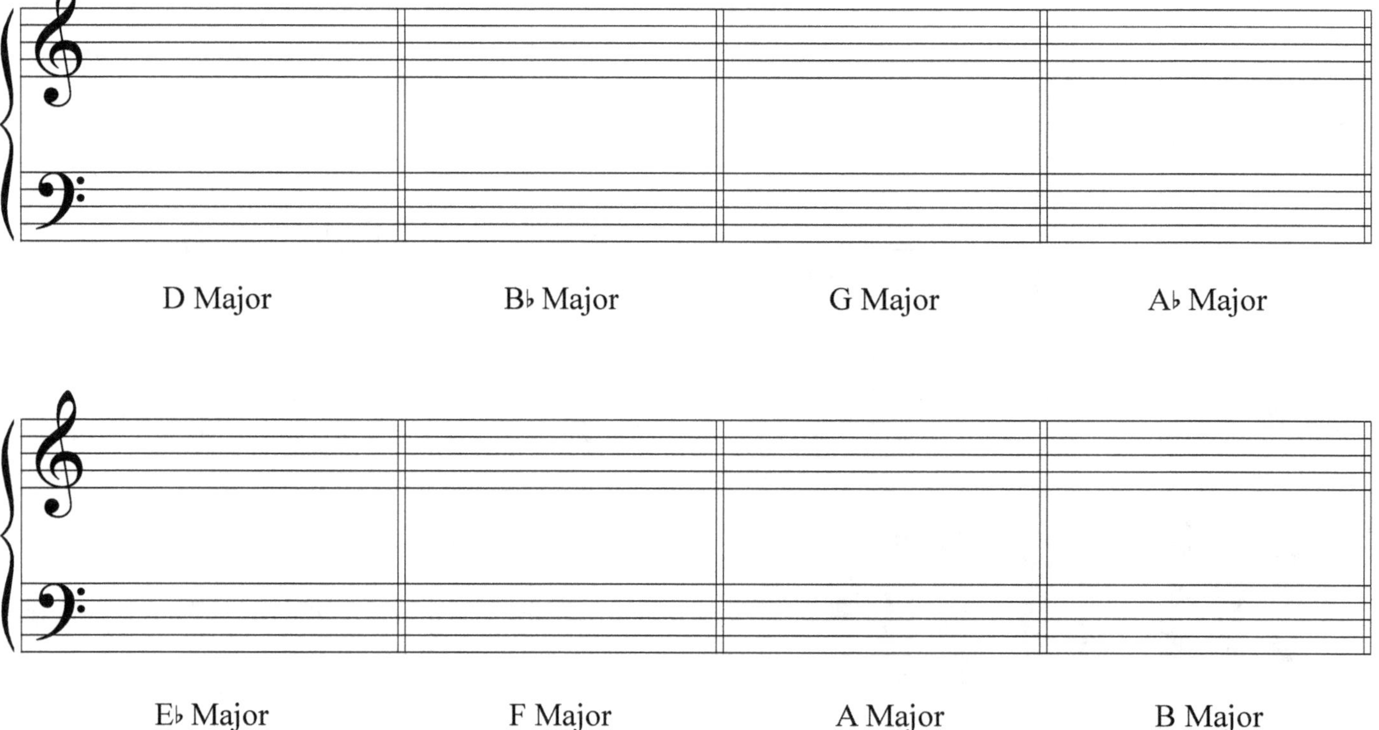

3. Circle the three notes in the scale below that make up a root position triad.

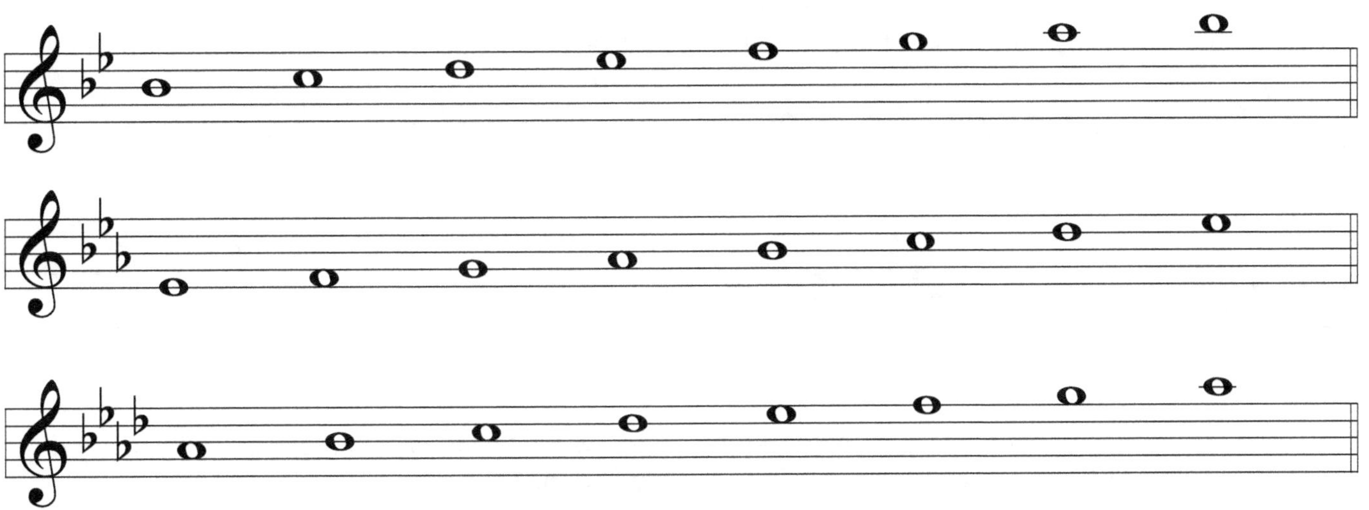

4. Each of these triads should have 3 notes (Do-Mi-Sol/root-middle-top).
<u>Fill in the missing note</u> to create a root position triad for the given key.

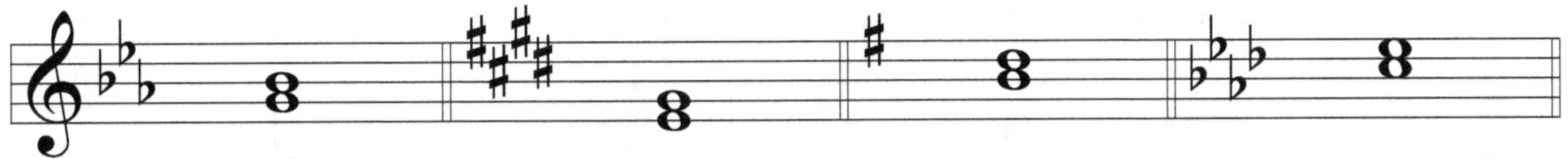

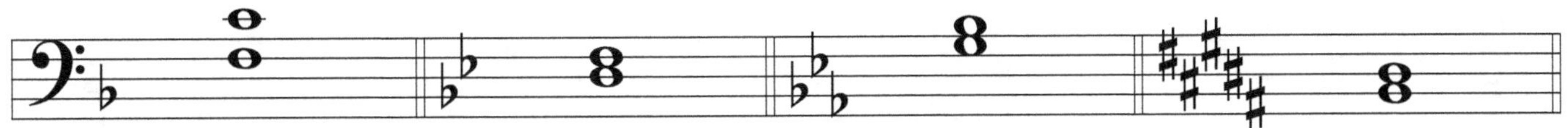

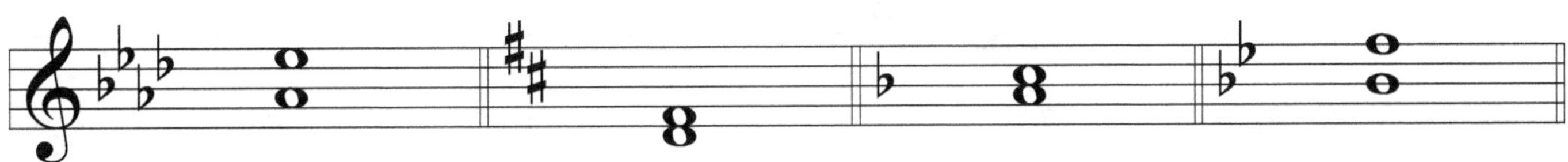

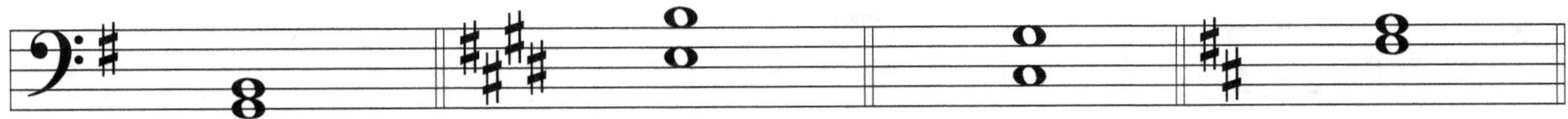

Review: Lessons 1-5

1. Name the following notes: Pay attention to the clefs & accidentals! The first one is done for you.

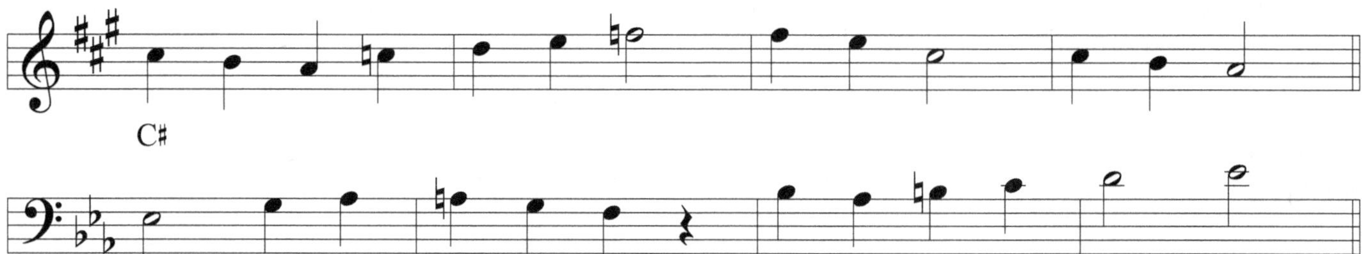

2. Draw a natural sign before each note on the staves below. Make sure the center part of the natural is on the same line or space as the note. The first one is done for you.

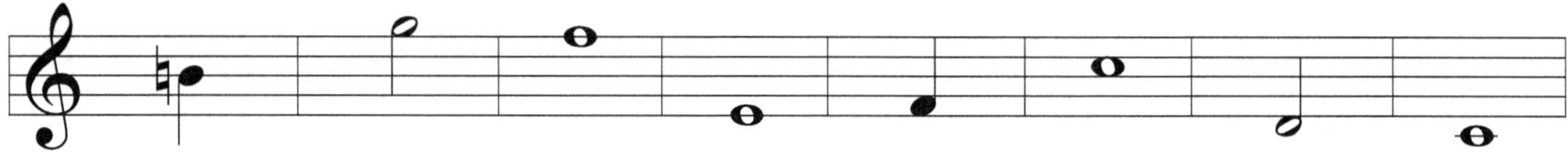

3. Draw a sharp sign before each note on the staves below. Make sure the center part of the sharp is on the same line or space as the note. The first one is done for you.

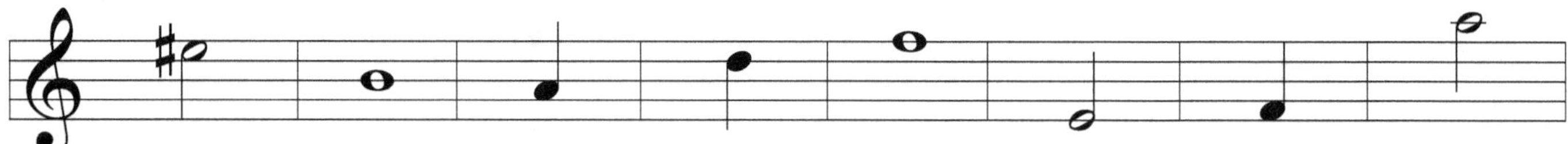

4. Draw a flat sign before each note on the staves below. Make sure the center part of the flat is on the same line or space as the note. The first one is done for you.

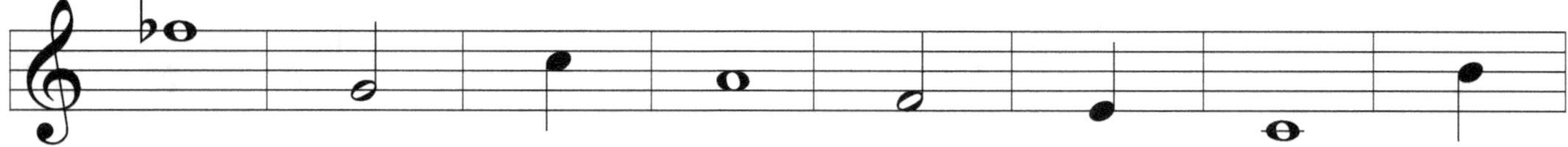

5. Name the note/rest and how many beats it has.

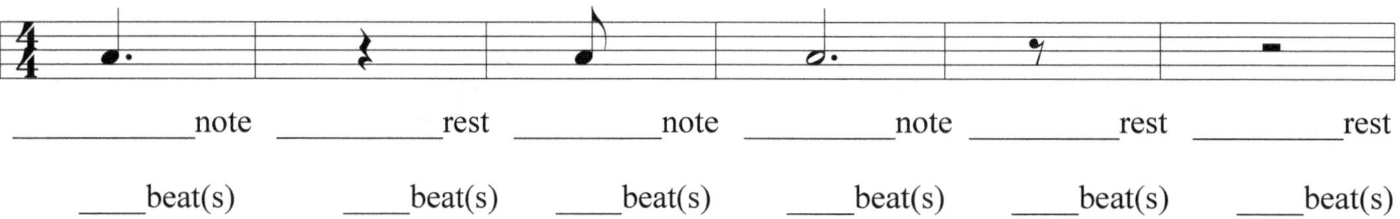

6. Check the correct counting for the example below.

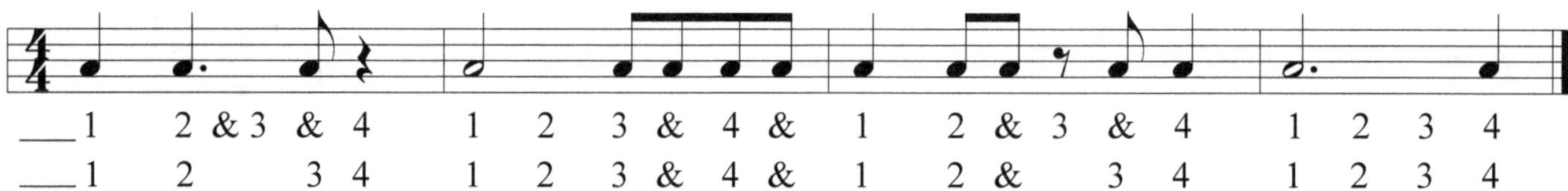

7. Write the beats under each note/rest in the following example.

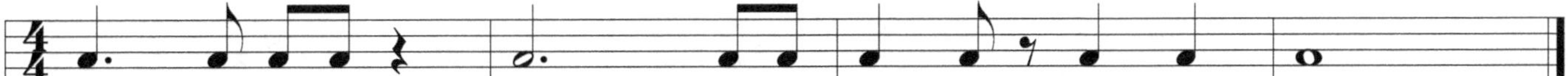

8. Add the 3 missing bar lines and a double bar line to the example below.

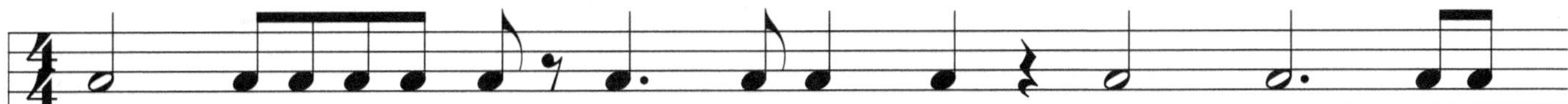

9. Add **one** missing note or rest to complete each measure in the example below.

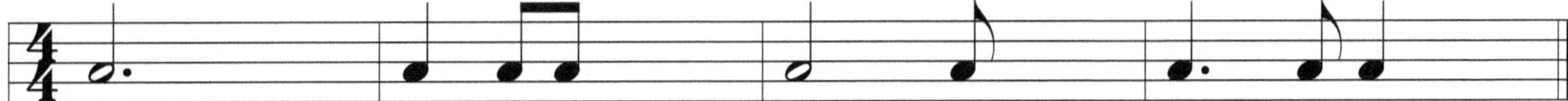

10. Write the letter name of each note.

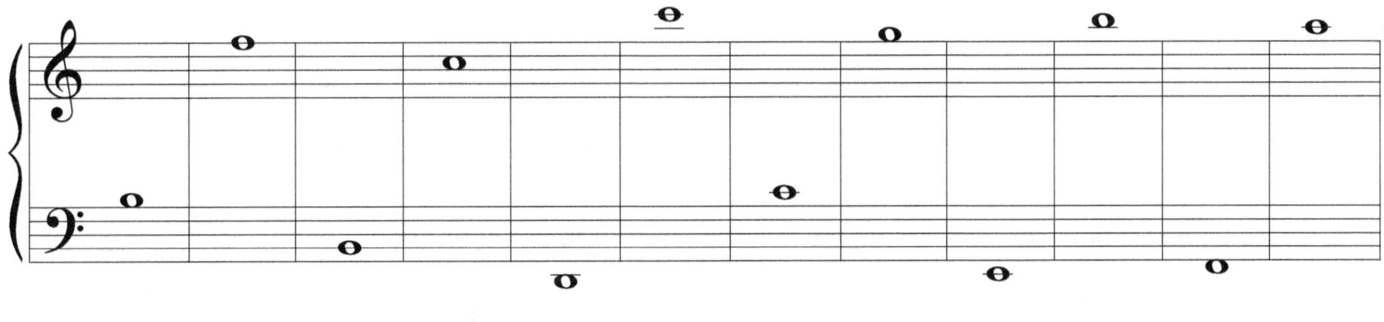

11. Add the necessary ♭'s to the scales below to create Major scales.

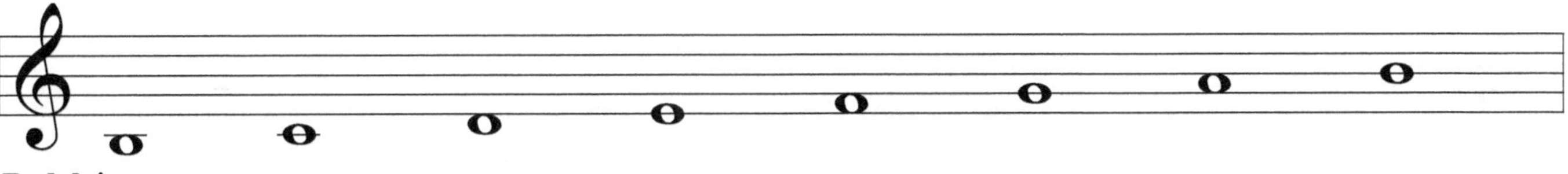

B♭ Maj.

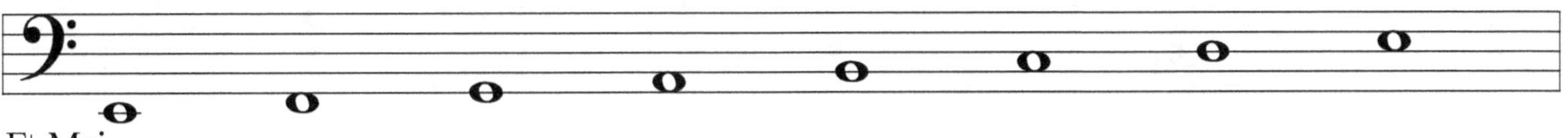

E♭ Maj.

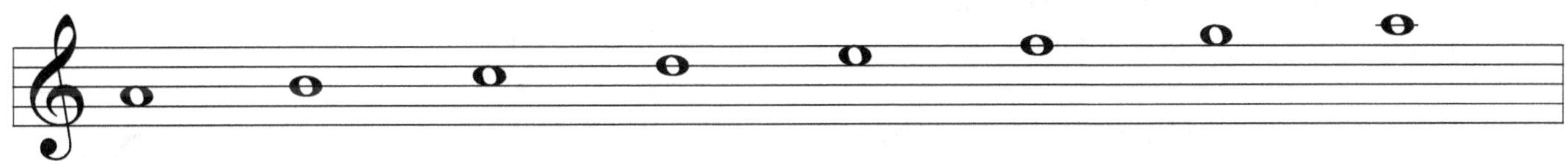

A♭ Maj.

12. Name the following triads. Remember, look at the bottom note (root) for the "name" of the triad.

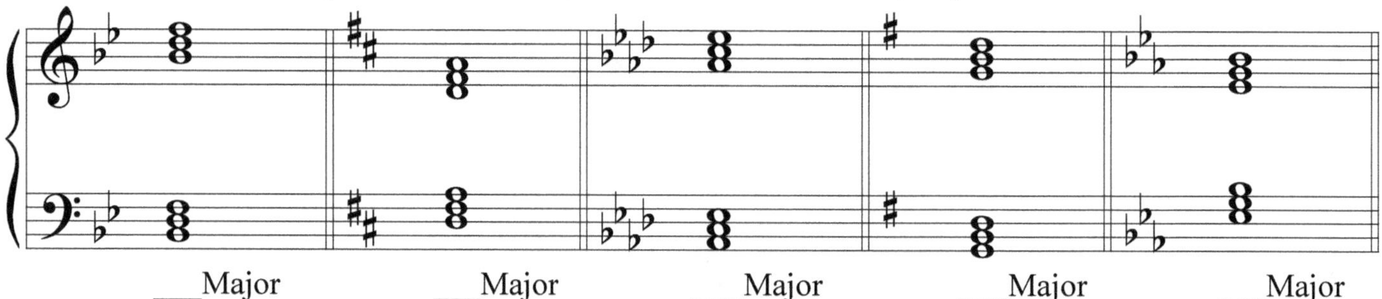

13. For the following examples, draw the correct key signature, then add the root position triads to both the Treble and Bass clefs. Look at question 12 for hints.

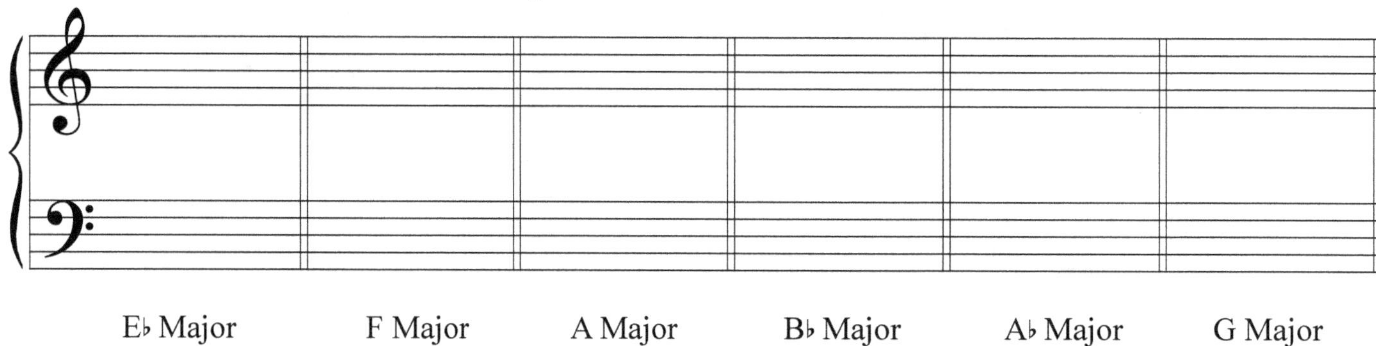

14. Circle the three notes in the scale below that make up a root position triad.

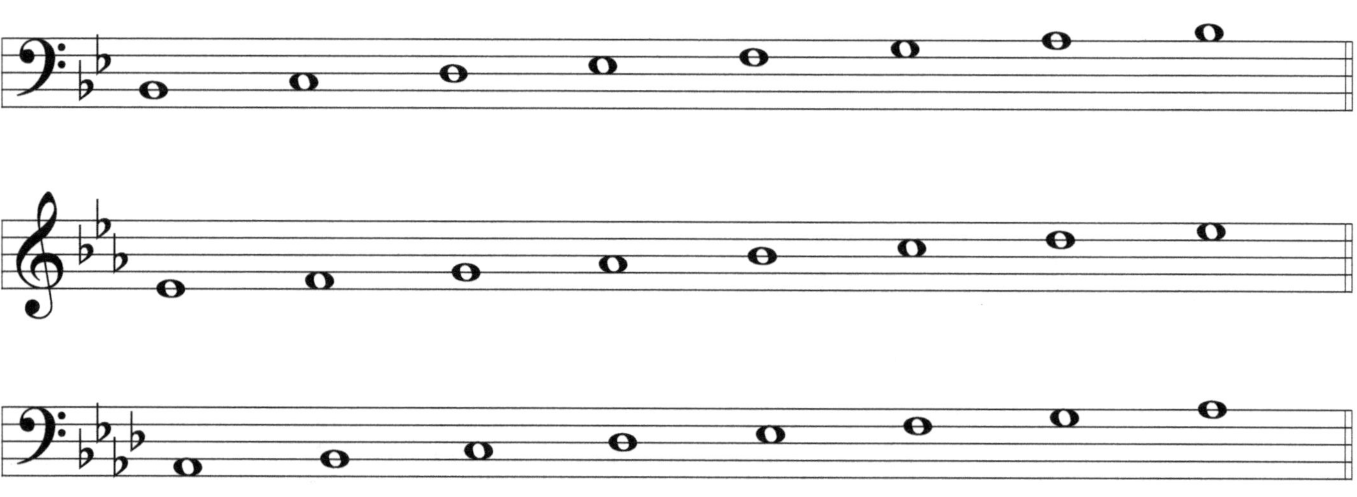

15. Each of these triads should have 3 notes (Do-Mi-Sol/root-middle-top). First, determine the key, then fill in the missing note to create a root position triad for the given key.

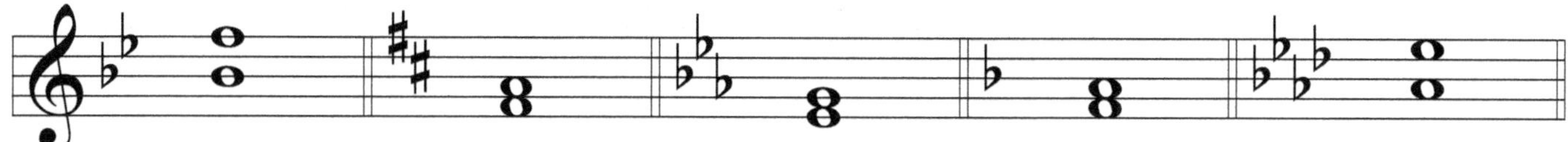

Lesson 6: Intervals (6ths & 7ths)

An Interval, in music, is the distance between any two notes. In this level, the intervals of a 6th and 7th will be covered. The intervals of a 2nd, 3rd, 4th & 5th were covered in Levels 1 & 2. **When counting intervals, be sure to include the bottom and top notes.**

For singing, Do-La is a 6th, Do-Ti is a 7th. Intervals are sung melodically (one note at a time), or harmonically (two notes at the same time - two singers singing at the same time).

Look at the examples below. Notice how the interval of a 6th has a line and a space note. The interval of a 7th either has 2 line notes or 2 space notes.

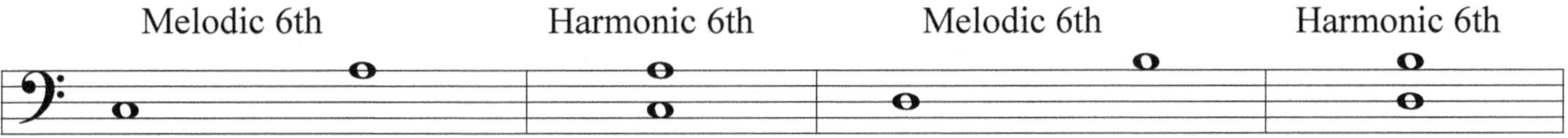

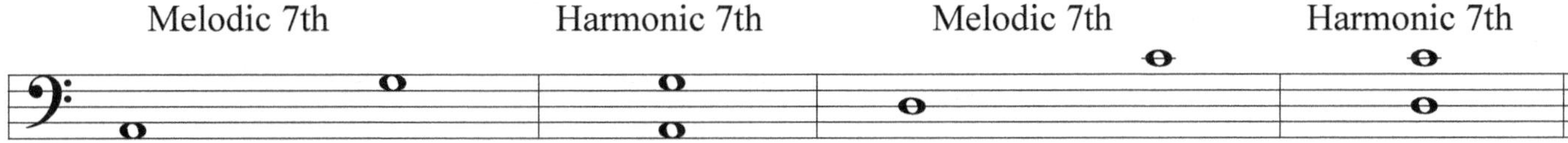

In singing, 2nds, 3rds, 4ths, 5ths, 6ths & 7ths use the following solfege.

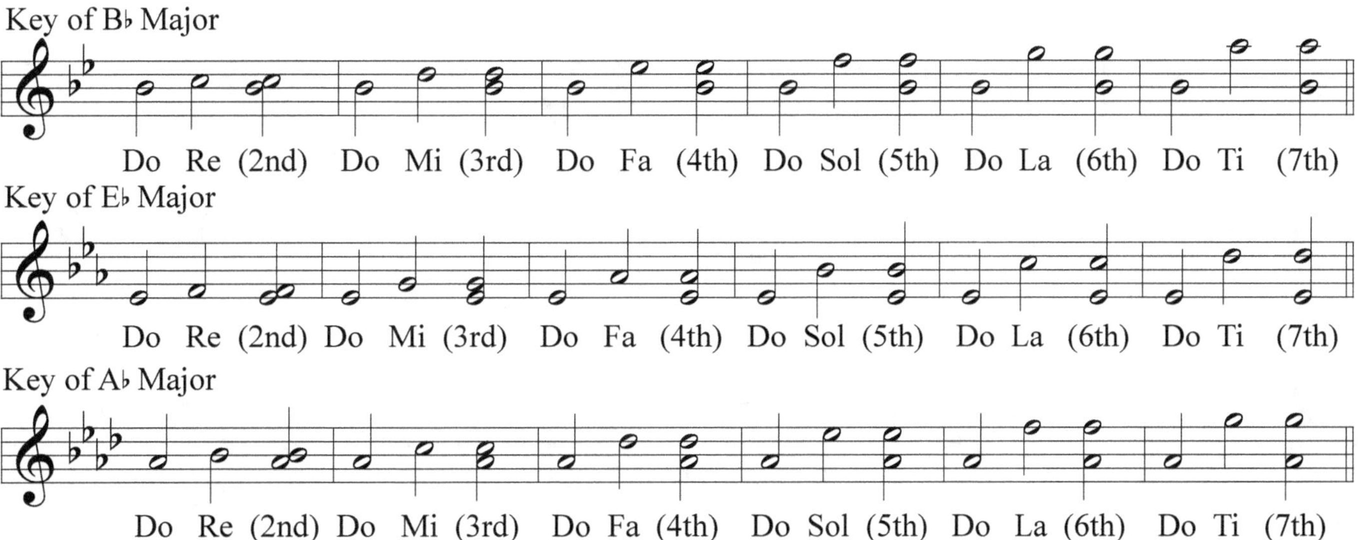

On the piano keyboard below, you can see the distance between the intervals. If you have a piano, keyboard, or piano app, play and sing these notes so you can hear the difference between the intervals.

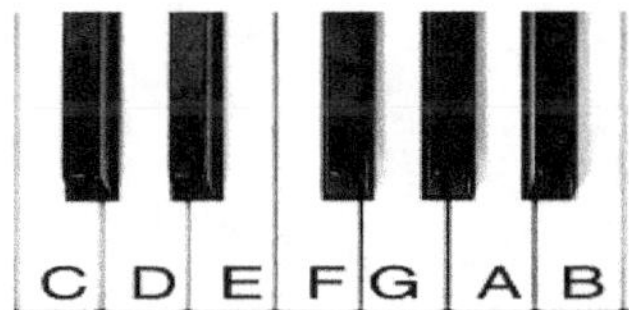

C-D is a 2nd C-E is a 3rd C-F is a 4th C-G is a 5th C-A is a 6th C-B is a 7th

Review: Lesson 6

1. Circle all of the harmonic 6ths.

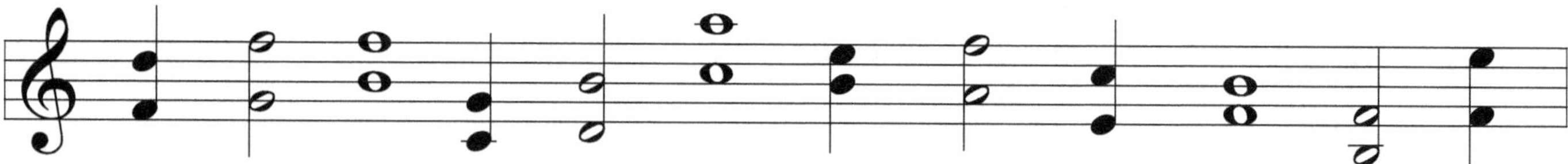

2. Circle all of the harmonic 7ths.

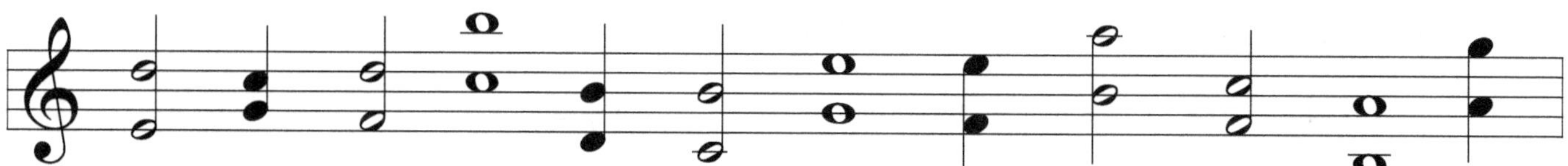

3. Label each melodic interval as a 6th or 7th.

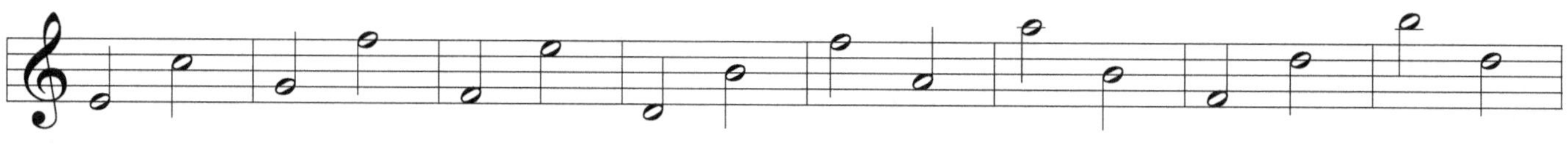

______ ______ ______ ______ ______ ______ ______ ______

4. Name each interval: 2nd, 3rd, 4th, 5th, 6th, or 7th.

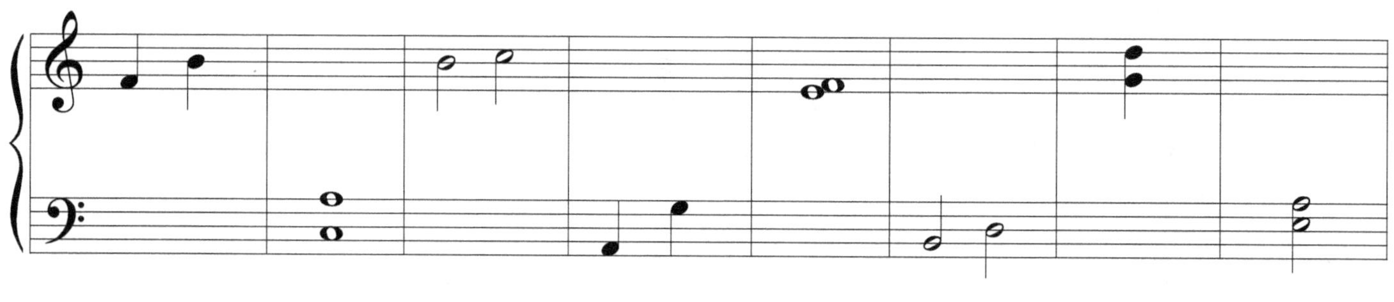

______ ______ ______ ______ ______ ______ ______ ______

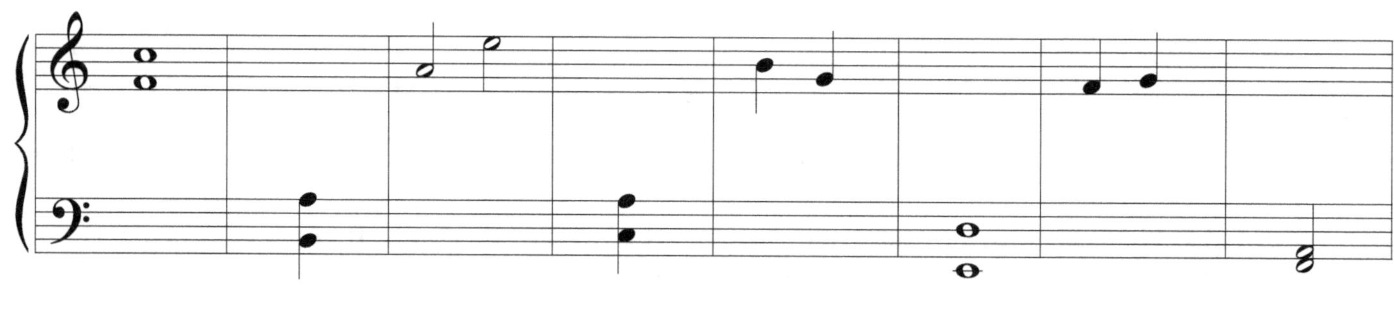

______ ______ ______ ______ ______ ______ ______ ______

5. Add one note per measure to complete the requested melodic intervals.
   Add the note after and above the given note. Make sure you add stems in the correct direction.
   Use half notes. The first one is done for you.

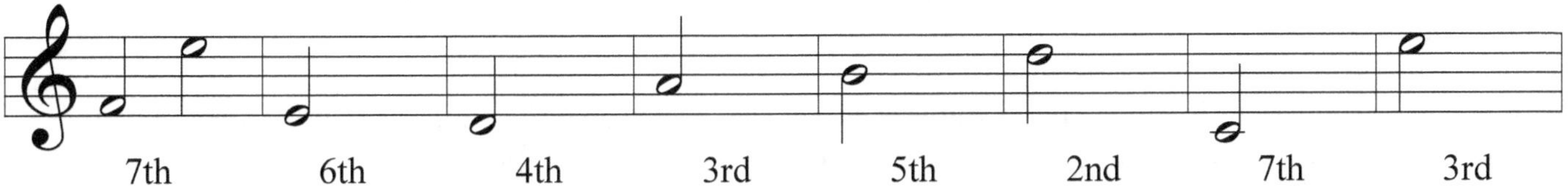

6. Add one note per measure to complete the requested melodic intervals.
   Add the note after and below the given note. Make sure you add stems in the correct direction.
   Use quarter notes. The first one is done for you.

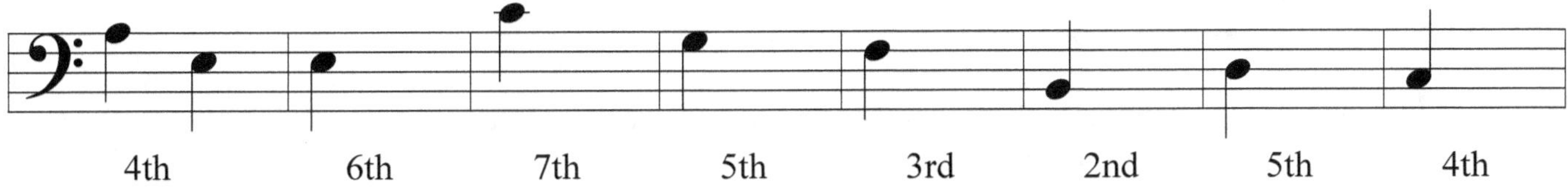

7. Add one note per measure to complete the requested harmonic intervals.
   Add the note above the given note. 2nds go above and next to the given note.
   Use whole notes. The first one is done for you.

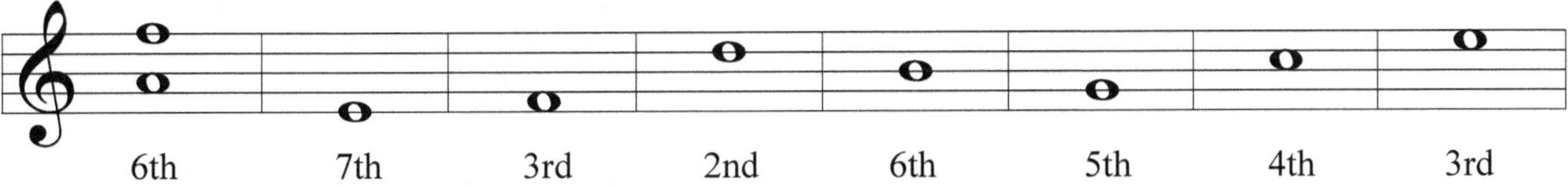

8. Add one note per measure to complete the requested harmonic intervals.
   Add the note below the given note. 2nds go below and next to the given note.
   Use whole notes. The first one is done for you.

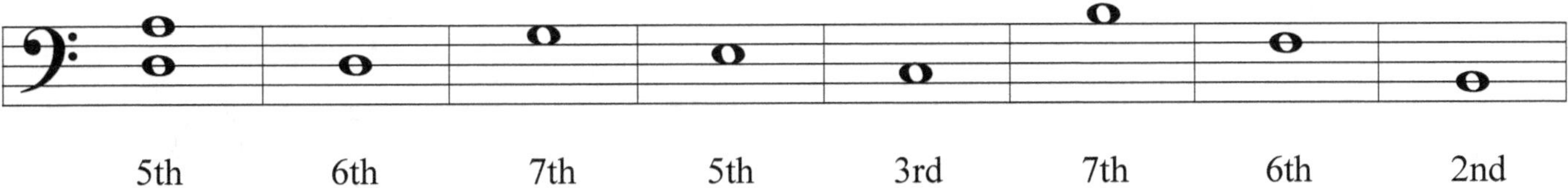

5th 6th 7th 5th 3rd 7th 6th 2nd

Lesson 7: Vocal Diction & IPA

Every time we sing a song, we are telling a story. As singers, we have to be exceptionally clear with how we pronounce the words of our songs, or our audience will not understand us and our story will not be told.

If you reference a dictionary in any Latin based language (English, Italian, French, German, Spanish, Latin, etc.) you will see some symbols next to the words. These symbols make up the International Phonetic Alphabet, or IPA. The IPA represents the sounds of a language. In fact, the IPA represents nearly any vowel or consonant made by human beings!

In this lesson, we'll focus on a few of the vowel sounds in the IPA. You will learn what the letter looks like in our language, what the IPA symbol for that letter is, and what it sounds like. The IPA symbols from Level 1-2 will also be in our chart on the following page.

Before we look at the symbols, make a couple of sounds so you can see all of the different positions your tongue moves to in order to make each sound.

Say "ah" as in the word "father," and "ee" as in the word "meet." You'll notice that when you say "ah," your tongue is at the bottom of your mouth, and when you say "ee" the center of your tongue moves to the roof of your mouth, while the tip remains down and behind the bottom teeth. When singing, we must be aware of any tension in our tongue, and ensure that it is in the proper position for creating accurate vowel sounds.

Here is a chart of the vowels we will learn in this lesson, along with their english equivalent.

æ	cat	[kæt]	Mid tongue, tip behind bottom teeth Lips slightly horizontal
ʊ	book	[bʊk]	Low tongue, tip below bottom teeth Lips relaxed
ʌ	strut	[strʌt]	Low tongue, tip behind bottom teeth Lips relaxed
ɔ	forest	[fɔrəst]	Low tongue, tip behind bottom teeth Lips slightly rounded

Courtesy of Sarah Sandvig

Practice saying the sounds above, and the english words in the second column.

Check that your tongue and lips are in the position described in the last column.

Additional IPA symbols, like the ones you see in the 3rd column will be introduced in later levels of these books.

Below is a chart of the vowels introduced in Levels 1 & 2, followed by the new vowels for this level.

Practice looking at each symbol, then say the english word and pay attention to the tongue and lips position described in the third column.

IPA SYMBOL	SOUND IN ENGLISH WORD	IPA SPELLING OF WORD	TONGUE/LIPS PLACEMENT
i	ski	[ski]	Center of tongue is high Lips relaxed
ɛ	led	[lɛd]	Low tongue Lips relaxed
ɑ	father	[ˈfɑðər]	Low tongue Lips relaxed
o	obey	[oʊˈbeɪ]	Low tongue, tip behind bottom teeth Rounded lips
u	goose	[gus]	Low tongue, tip behind bottom teeth Rounded lips
ɪ	kit	[kɪt]	High tongue, sides touching top teeth Lips relaxed
e	ate	[eɪt]	High tongue, sides touching top teeth Lips relaxed
ə	afraid	[əˈfreɪd]	Mid tongue, tip behind bottom teeth Lips relaxed
æ	cat	[kæt]	Mid tongue, tip behind bottom teeth Lips slightly horizontal
ʊ	book	[bʊk]	Low tongue, tip below bottom teeth Lips relaxed & slightly pouted
ʌ	strut	[strʌt]	Low tongue, tip behind bottom teeth Lips relaxed
ɔ	forest	[fɔrəst]	Low tongue, tip behind bottom teeth Lips slightly rounded

Courtesy of Sarah Sandvig

Review: Lesson 7

1. Check the English word that contains the same sound as the given IPA symbol.

e	___Bet ___Late	u	___Food ___Cup	ɑ	___Pat ___Caught	i	___Bite ___Meet
ə	___Supply ___Best	ɪ	___Fit ___Bite	o	___Boat ___Pot	ɛ	___Bless ___Creep
ʌ	___Cut ___Bound	ʊ	___Flute ___Look	æ	___Bat ___Fate	ɔ	___Thought ___Boot

2. Circle the correct answer for the proper tongue and lip position for each IPA symbol. Say each sound, it will help!

ʌ - Tongue is - high- and lips are - relaxed -
- low - - rounded -

ʊ - Tongue is - high- and lips are - relaxed -
- low - - rounded -

æ - Tongue is - high- and lips are - relaxed -
- low - - rounded -

ə - Tongue is - high- and lips are - relaxed -
- low - - rounded -

i - Tongue is - high- and lips are - relaxed -
- low - - rounded -

ɔ - Tongue is - high- and lips are - relaxed -
- low - - rounded -

3. Write a word in the blank provided that uses the given IPA sound. Don't use any of the words from above or on the previous page!

ʌ________________	e________________	o________________
ʊ________________	ɪ________________	i________________
ə________________	ɑ________________	ɛ________________
æ________________	u________________	ɔ________________

Lesson 8: Sight-Singing

In order to learn a song, singers learn to read both rhythmic patterns and notes (melody) on the staff. Singing a melody for the first time is called "sight-singing." Below are some rhythmic examples using the notes introduced so far.

Hint: When singing rhythmic examples, take a breath on the rests: then you won't miss them! *Tap* and *say* the beats, then sing the examples on a La (choose any pitch that suits your voice).

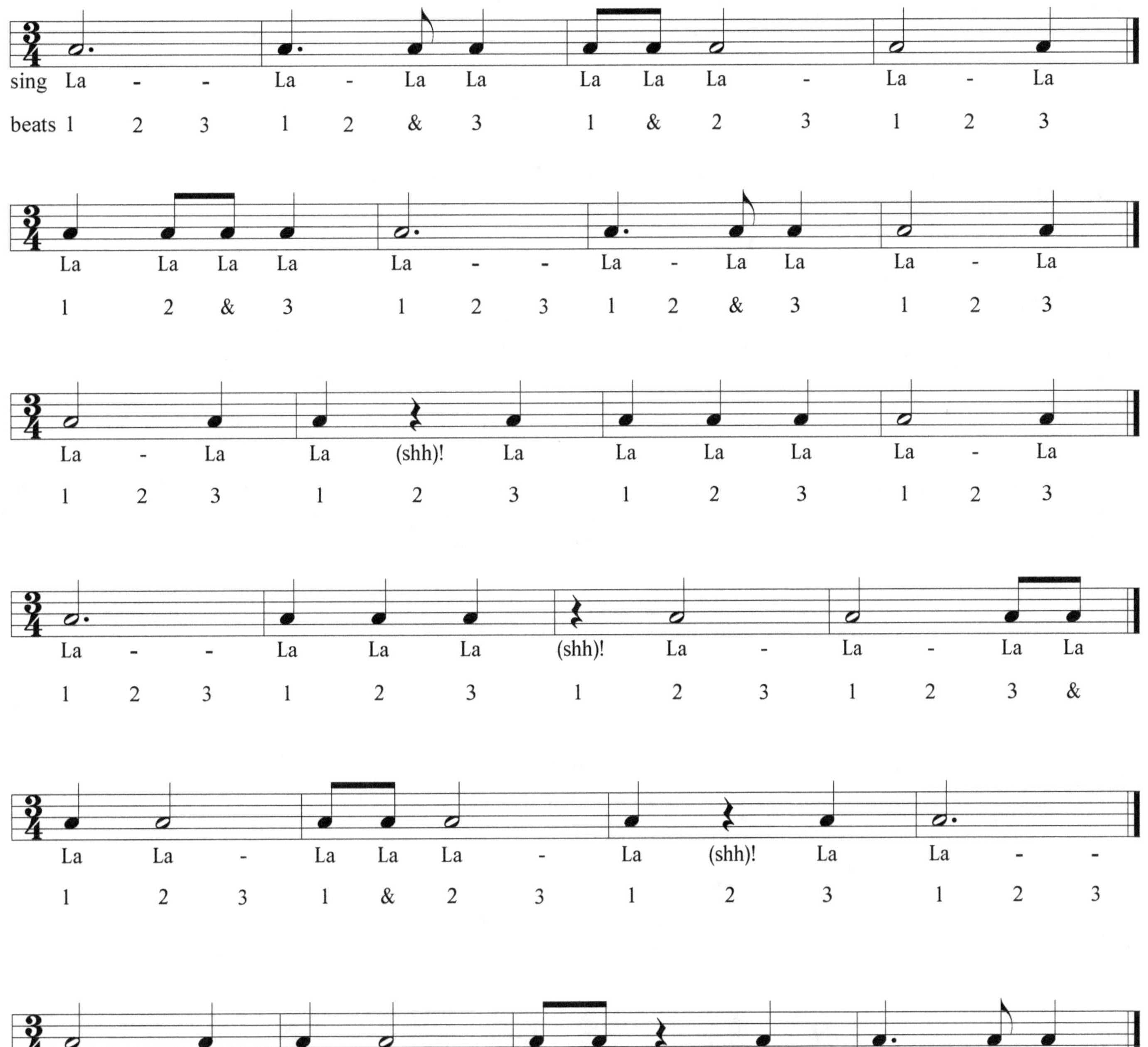

Melody & Solfege

Solfege is a system of assigning a syllable to each note of a scale, just like in the song "Do-Re-Mi" from the musical *The Sound of Music*.

Solfege is a useful tool when sight-singing. Moveable "Do" is when "Do" matches the **root** of whatever key you're in. The following examples contain a Major scale in the three keys covered in this level.

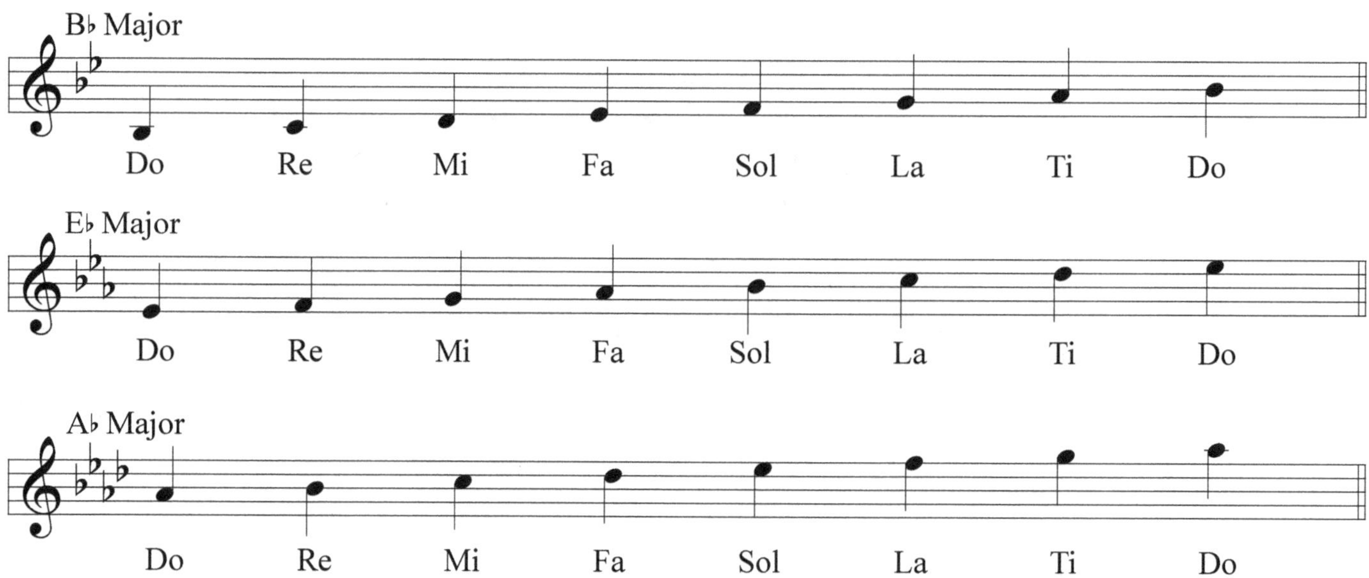

In this Level, you'll learn to sing melodies with Do, Re, Mi, Fa & Sol. The following melodies have the solfege written under the notes for you. Pay attention to the key signature changes. Use the picture of the piano below to find your starting note on your piano or piano app.

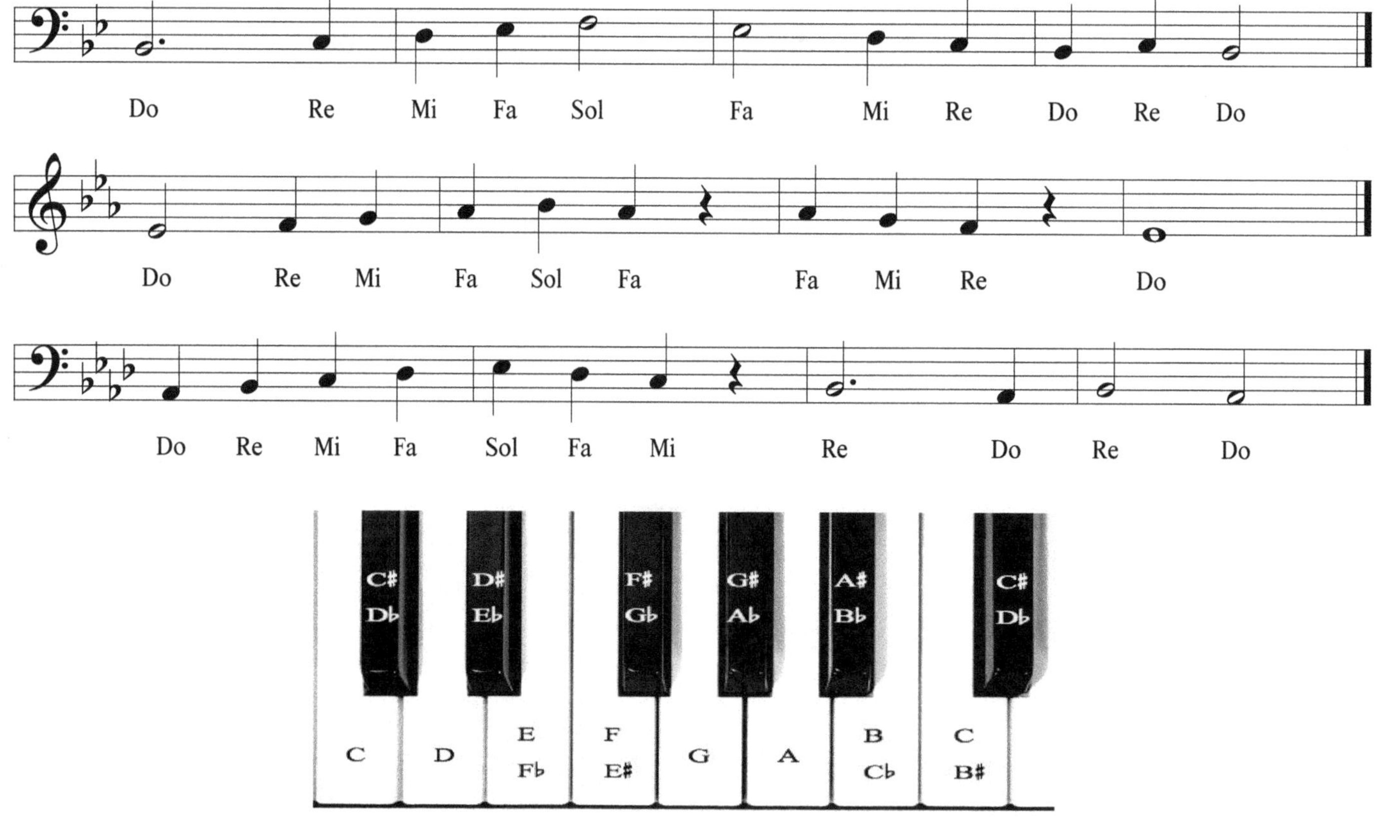

Review: Lesson 8

1. For the following melodies, write the note names, solfege & beats underneath the notes. Practice singing the examples when you are done!

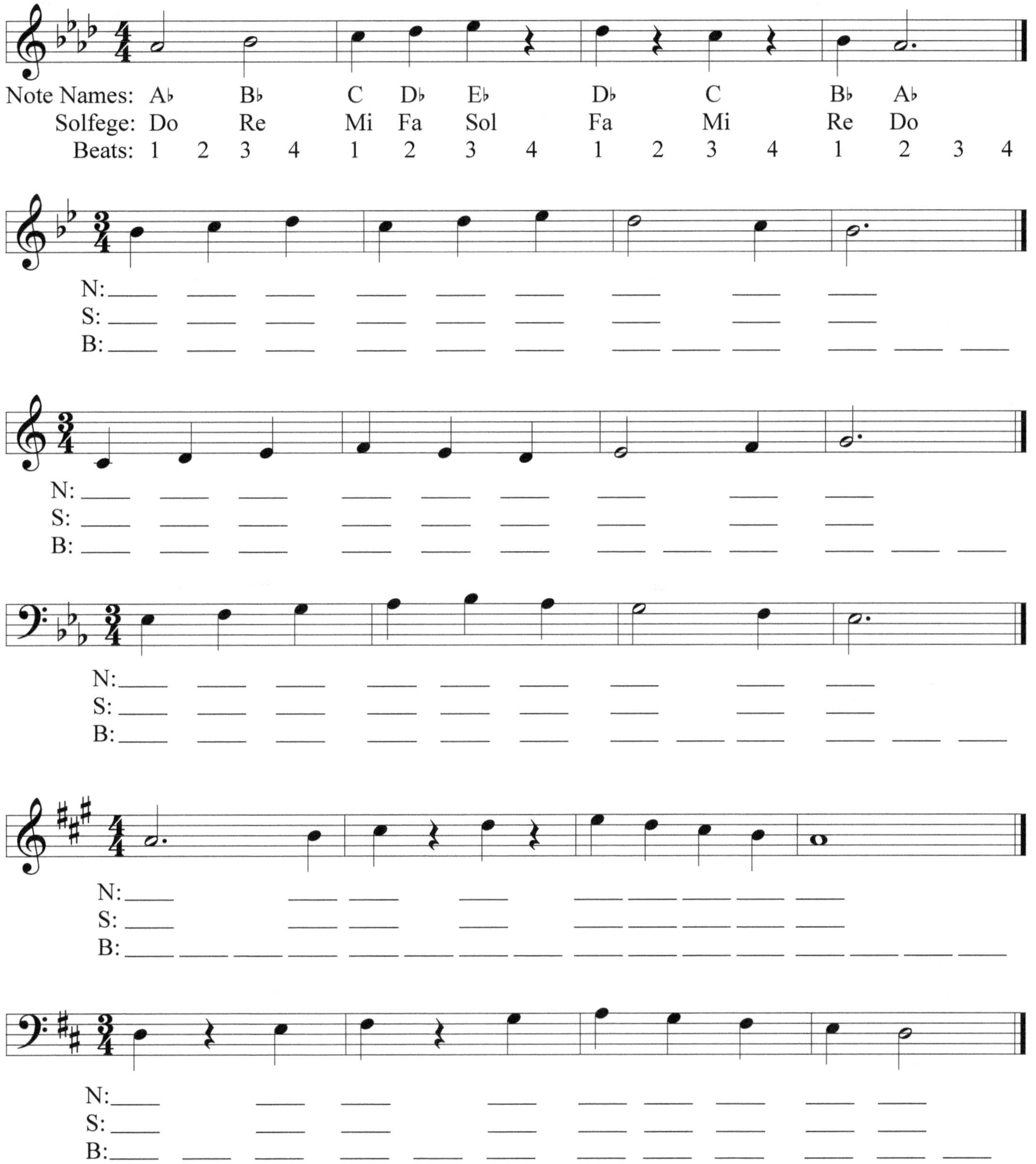

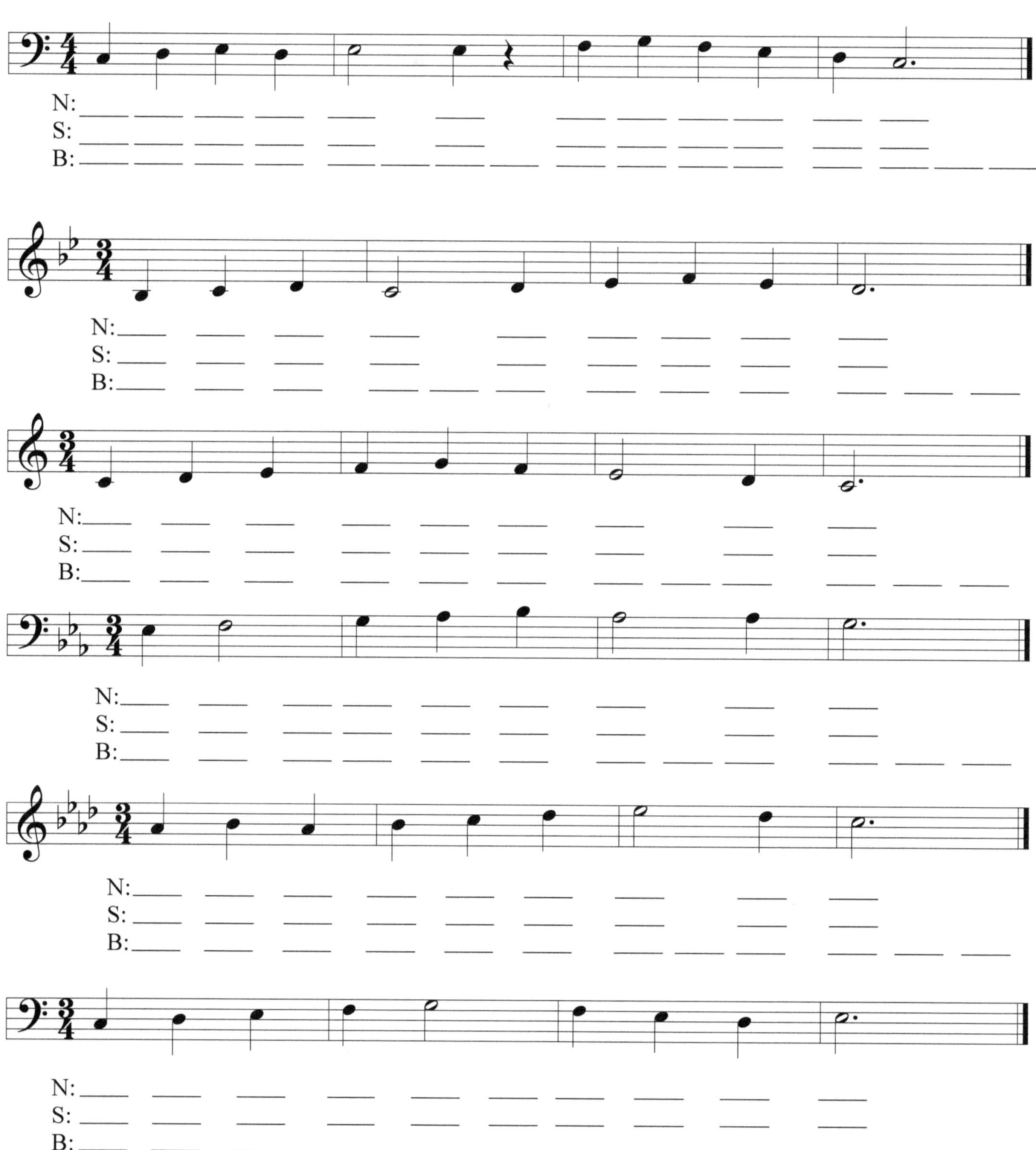
N:
S:
B:
N:
S:
B:
N:
S:
B:
N:
S:
B:
N:
S:
B:
N:
S:
B:

Lesson 9: Musical Terms

A crucial part of understanding music is being able to recognize and define musical terms. Below is a list of terms covered in this level.

accidental - a flat, sharp, or natural sign

allegro - a lively, fast tempo

andante - a moderate, graceful, walking tempo

broken triad - three consecutive tones, Do-Mi-Sol

Classical period of music - a general term for the style of music written between 1750 and 1820

diminuendo (*dim.*) - gradually getting softer

dolce - sweetly

IPA- the International Phonetic Alphabet: a standard representation of the sounds of spoken language

lento - slow

moderato - moderate tempo

molto - very

Musical Theatre/Broadway - a 20th Century form of theatre, combining music, songs, spoken dialogue and dance

natural (♮) - cancels the effect of a previous flat or sharp

poco a poco - little by little

sforzando (*sfz*) - a heavy, strong accent

simple meter - a time signature in which the basic beat can be divided by two

Review: Lesson 9

1. Check the appropriate answer for each of the following questions.

a. What is the name for a sharp, flat or natural sign?

____dynamic

____accidental

b. Which term means to gradually get softer?

____diminuendo

____crescendo

c. This Italian term means "very."

____dolce

____molto

d. This sign cancels the effect of a previous flat or sharp.

____forte

____natural

e. This Italian term means "little by little."

____poco a poco

____dolce

f. This period of music refers to the style of music written between the years of 1750-1820.

____Renaissance Period

____Classical Period

g. This Italian word means a "moderate, graceful, walking tempo."

____Allegro

____Andante

h. This Italian word means "lively," or "fast."

____Allegro

____Andante

i. This Italian word means "sweetly."

____dolce

____molto

j. A broken triad consists of which three tones?

____Do-Mi-Do

____Do-Mi-Sol

2. Complete the following crossword puzzle using the terms from this level.

Level 3 Crossword

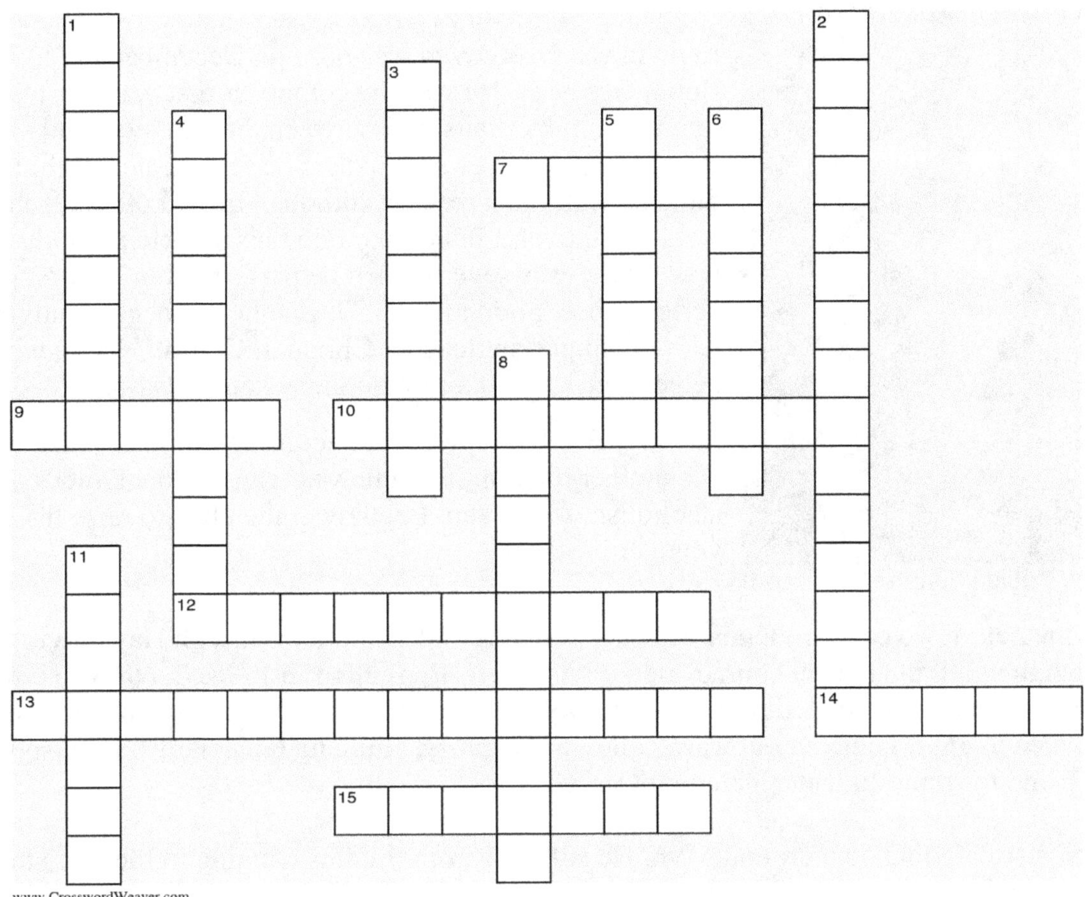

ACROSS

7 slow
9 very
10 a flat, sharp, or natural sign
12 gradually getting softer
13 also known as Broadway- a 20th Century form of theatre, combining music, songs, spoken dialogue and dance (two words)
14 sweetly
15 a lively, fast tempo

DOWN

1 a heavy, strong accent
2 a general term for the style of music written between 1750 and 1820 (two words)
3 little by little (three words)
4 three consecutive tones, Do-Mi-Sol (two words)
5 a moderate, graceful, walking tempo
6 moderate tempo
8 a time signature in which the basic beat can be divided by two (two words)
11 cancels the effect of a previous flat or sharp

crossword created at:
www.CrosswordWeaver.com

Lesson 10: Spotlight on Composers

An important part of music education is learning about the history of music. Studying composers allows for understanding the music we sing and why it was written the way it was. In this level you will learn about Ludwig van Beethoven and Johann Sebastian Bach.

LUDWIG VAN BEETHOVEN

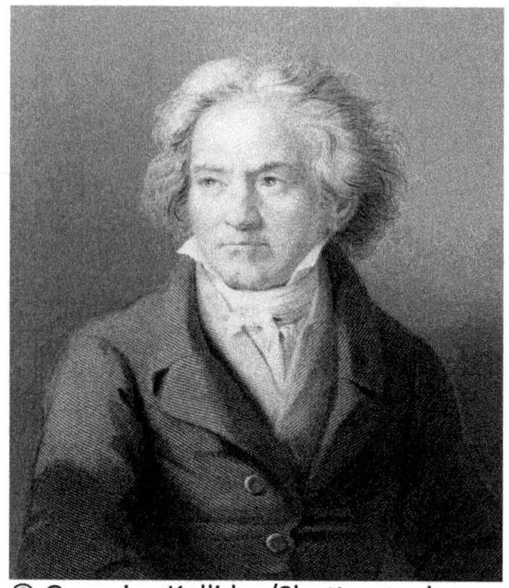
© Georgios Kollidas/Shutterstock.com

Ludwig van Beethoven was born on December 17, 1770 in Bonn, Germany. He was the composer that was most important in the transition between the Classical and Romantic periods of music; thus he represented both. His father was his first teacher, although he had other teachers as well. Beethoven's father exploited his son claiming that he was six (he was seven) when he performed in his first public performance. Soon after 1779, Beethoven began studying with the important teacher Christian Gottlob Neefe, who helped him write his first published composition.

In 1787, Beethoven went to Vienna and possibly met Mozart. His mother died in this same year causing his father's alcoholism to worsen. Beethoven then had to raise his two younger brothers.

He spent the next few years in Vienna studying counterpoint with Franz Joseph Haydn, violin with Schuppanzigh and Italian vocal composition with Salieri. Beginning in 1798, Beethoven wrote some of his most famous works including his first symphony and "Moonlight Sonata" (the latter of which was dedicated to a girl he loved but wasn't allowed to marry, Giulietta Guicciardi). He also began teaching piano to some students, including Carl Czerny.

Beethoven started going deaf around 1796. He suffered from tinnitus (ringing in the ears) making it hard for him to have conversations. The source of his hearing loss is unknown. At the end of the premiere of his Ninth Symphony, Beethoven, who was conducting, had to be turned around to see the applause of the audience because he couldn't hear it. Beethoven used conversation books to communicate with his friends.

Beethoven's only opera, *Fidelio* premiered in 1805, and he wrote two masses and several vocal pieces. Perhaps his most famous vocal piece is the chorus from the Ninth Symphony, called "Ode to Joy." The text for this chorus is from Schiller's poem and talks about the brotherhood of humanity. Beethoven died on March 26, 1827. His funeral was attended by 20,000 people.

Best Known Scores & Songs:
Immortal Beloved- 1994 (movie), ***Eroica-*** 2003 (movie), ***Copying Beethoven-*** 2006 (movie)

An die ferne Geliebte- 1816 (song cycle), ***25 Scottish Songs Opus 108, Fidelio-*** 1814 (opera)

Beethoven wrote hundreds of vocal songs, song cycles and choral pieces. He also wrote nine symphonies, nine concertos, five piano concertos, sixteen string quartets, twelve piano trios, and a plethora of chamber music.

JOHANN SEBASTIAN BACH

Johann Sebastian Bach was born in the Baroque period of music on March 31, 1685 in Eisenach, Germany. His father taught him how to play violin and harpsichord. Both of Bach's parents died in 1694, so at 10 years old he moved in with his oldest brother, Johann Christoph Bach. Johann taught Bach how to play the clavichord. When he was 14, he was given a choral scholarship to study at St. Michael's School in Lüneburg.

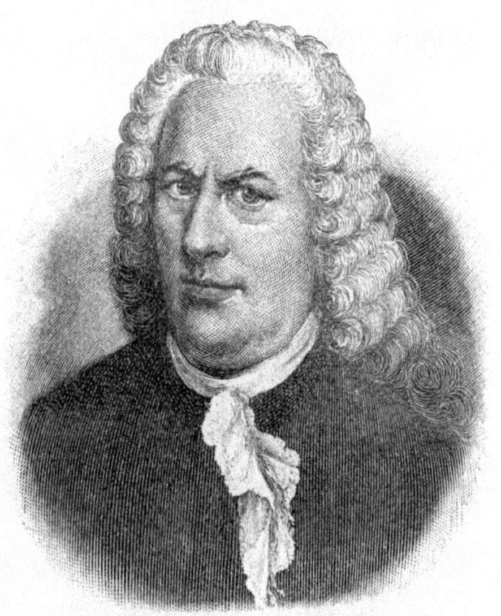

© Nicku/Shutterstock.com

In 1703, Bach accepted a job as organist at St. Boniface's Church in Arnstadt. It was here that he began composing organ preludes and worked to refine his contrapuntal technique. In 1706, Bach took a new job as organist at St. Blasius's in Muhlhausen. He married his second cousin, Maria Barbara Bach that same year. They had seven children including Carl Phillip Emanuel Bach and Wilhelm Friedemann Bach, who became famous composers.

Bach took a job in Weimer as organist and concertmaster less than a year after beginning his previous job in Muhlhausen. It was in Weimer that Bach wrote some of his most famous keyboard and orchestral works. Most of his pieces were written for organ and harpsichord. His most well-known keyboard pieces from this period included *Das Wohltemperierte Clavier* (The well-tempered keyboard), and the "Little Organ Book" written for his son Wilhelm, which contains traditional Lutheran Chorales (hymns).

In 1717, Prince Leopold hired Bach to be the director of music. He composed the well-known *Brandenburg Concertos* during this time. In 1720, Bach's wife suddenly died, but he met and married the soprano Anna Magdalena Wilcke the following year. They had 13 more children, 3 of whom also became composers.

From 1723-1750, Bach held the position as Cantor of the Thomasschule at St. Thomas Church in Leipzig, as well as Director of Music in the main churches in town. During this time, he wrote Lutheran Hymns (chorales) for the church as well as cantatas, fugues, preludes, toccatas, masses & motets. He used "counterpoint," a technique of writing music where two or more melodies interact at the same time, for much of his composing. Bach passed away on June 28, 1750. He wrote hundreds of vocal pieces that are still performed today. His composition style influenced several famous composers including Beethoven and Mozart.

Best Known Vocal Works:
Mass in B minor, Magnificat, Easter Oratorio, Christmas Oratorio, Hymns & Chorales

Other Significant Works:
The Art of the Fugue, The Brandenburg Concertos, The Well-Tempered Clavier, Notebook for Anna Magdalena Bach

Review: Lesson 10

1. Fill in the correct answer(s) to the following questions about Ludwig van Beethoven & Johann Sebastian Bach

Ludwig van Beethoven

a. Ludwig van Beethoven was born in which country?____________________________

b. He represents both the ____________________________ and ________________________ periods of music.

c. Who was his first piano teacher? _____________________________________

d. He suffered the physical handicap of ____________________________.

e. Which of his symphonies has a chorus in the last movement ?____________________________

f. What is the name of the 1994 film about Beethoven? ___________________________________

Johann Sebastian Bach

a. Johann Sebastian Bach was born in which country? ____________________________

b. He represents the _________________________ period of music.

c. What is the main type of technique he used to write his keyboard music, in which two or more melodies interact simultaneously? ______________________________________

d. How many children did Bach have in total? ___________________

e. What is the name of the short vocal piece type that Bach wrote for the Lutheran church?____

f. Name the two main keyboard instruments that Bach played.____________________________ &_____________________________________

Level 3 Review Test

Answer the questions about the following musical example. (16 points)

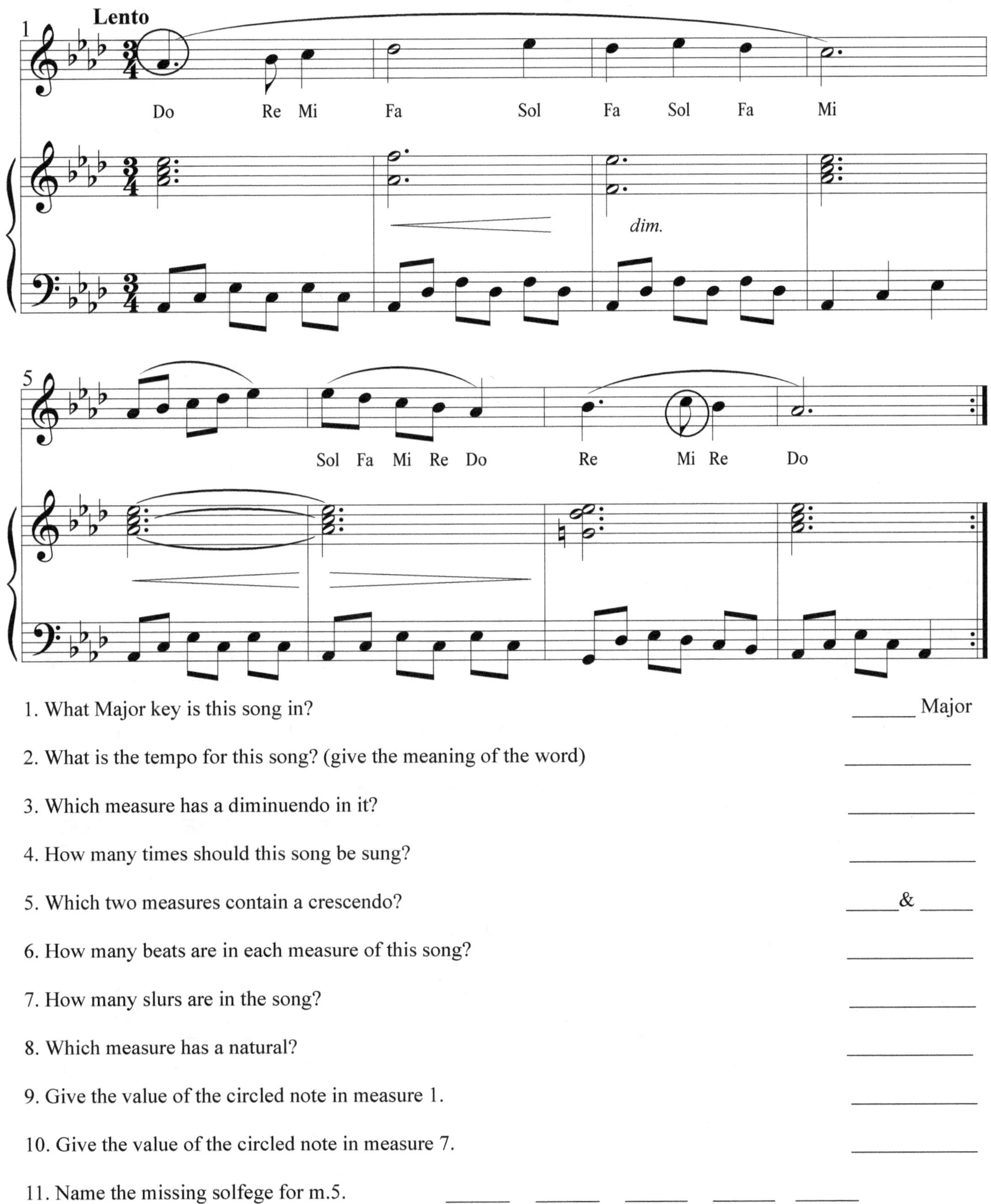

1. What Major key is this song in? ______ Major
2. What is the tempo for this song? (give the meaning of the word) ____________
3. Which measure has a diminuendo in it? ____________
4. How many times should this song be sung? ____________
5. Which two measures contain a crescendo? _____& _____
6. How many beats are in each measure of this song? ____________
7. How many slurs are in the song? ____________
8. Which measure has a natural? ____________
9. Give the value of the circled note in measure 1. ____________
10. Give the value of the circled note in measure 7. ____________
11. Name the missing solfege for m.5. ______ ______ ______ ______ ______

12. Name the following notes. (16 points)

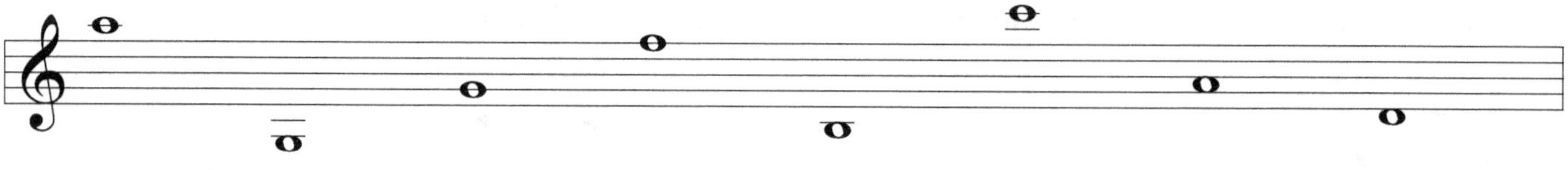

____ ____ ____ ____ ____ ____ ____ ____

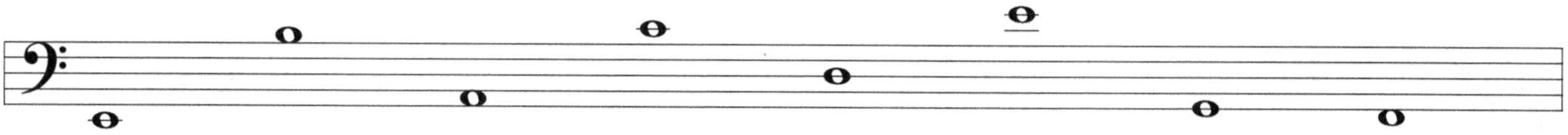

____ ____ ____ ____ ____ ____ ____ ____

13. Name the following notes and their values *(for example: Quarter note, 1 beat).* (12 points)

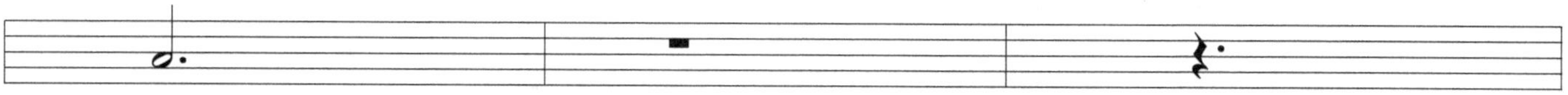

________________note/____beat(s) ____________rest/____beat(s) ________________rest/____beat(s)

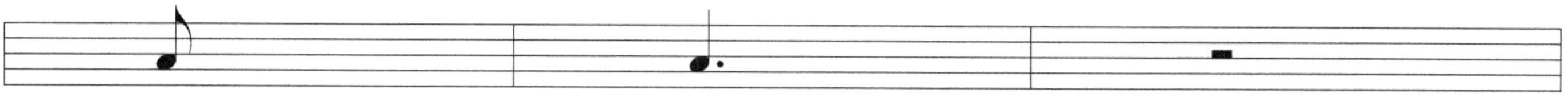

________________note/____beat(s) __________________note/____beat(s) ________________rest/____beat(s)

14. Add 3 bar lines and a double bar line to the following example. (4 points)

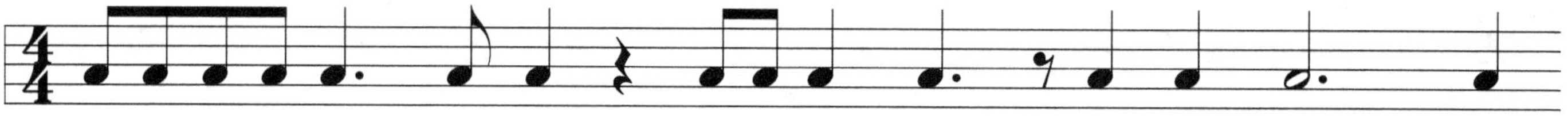

15. Add the missing time signature, then write the beats underneath the notes. (5 points-one for time signature, one for each correct measure)

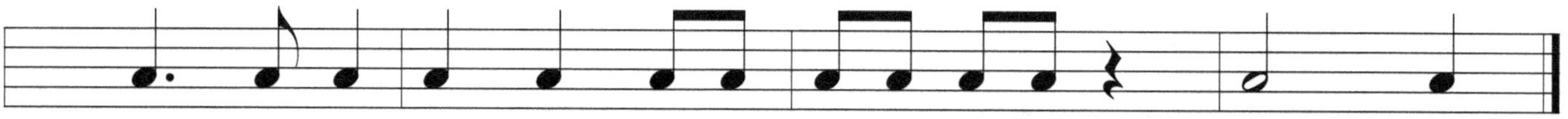

16. Name the key signature and interval (6th/7th) for each example. (8 points)

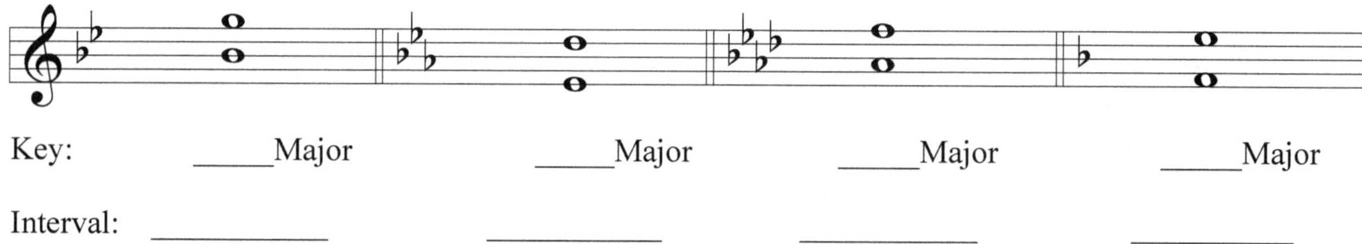

Key: _____Major _____Major _____Major _____Major

Interval: ___________ ___________ ___________ ___________

17. Each of these chords should have a Do (1), Mi (3), & Sol (5).
Fill in the missing note for each chord in both clefs to create a root position triad. (8 points)

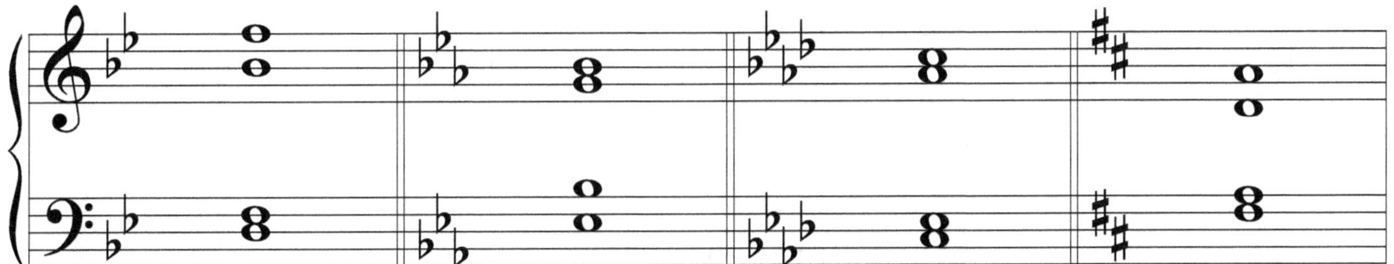

18. Draw a whole note above the given note to create the requested harmonic intervals. (8 points)

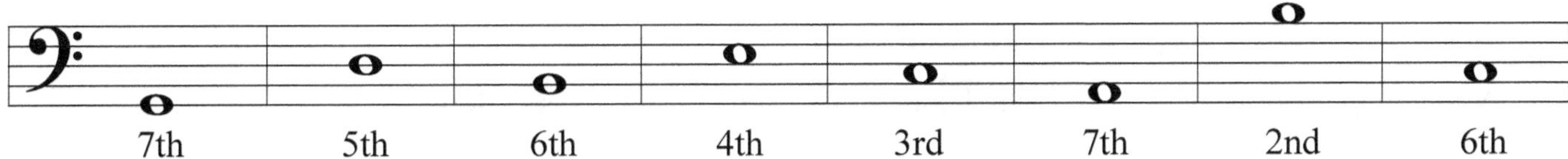

19. Write the beats under the examples. Pay attention to the time signatures!
(8 points- 1 point per correct measure)

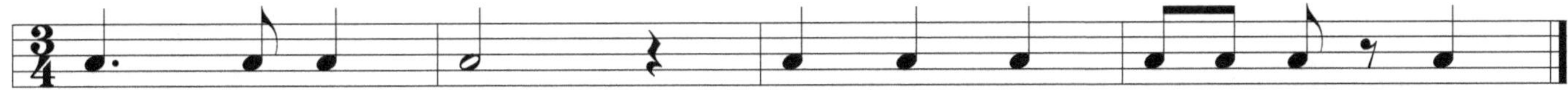

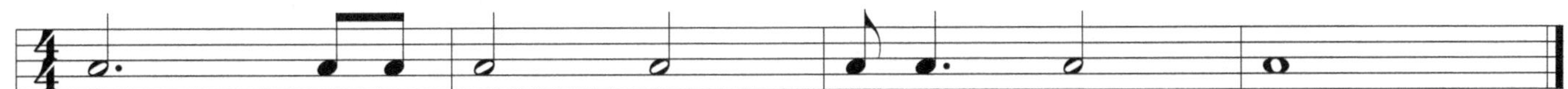

20. Write the note names and solfege directly under each note in the following examples. Don't forget to add ♭'s if needed. (8 points-1 point per correct measure: both solfege and notes must be correct)

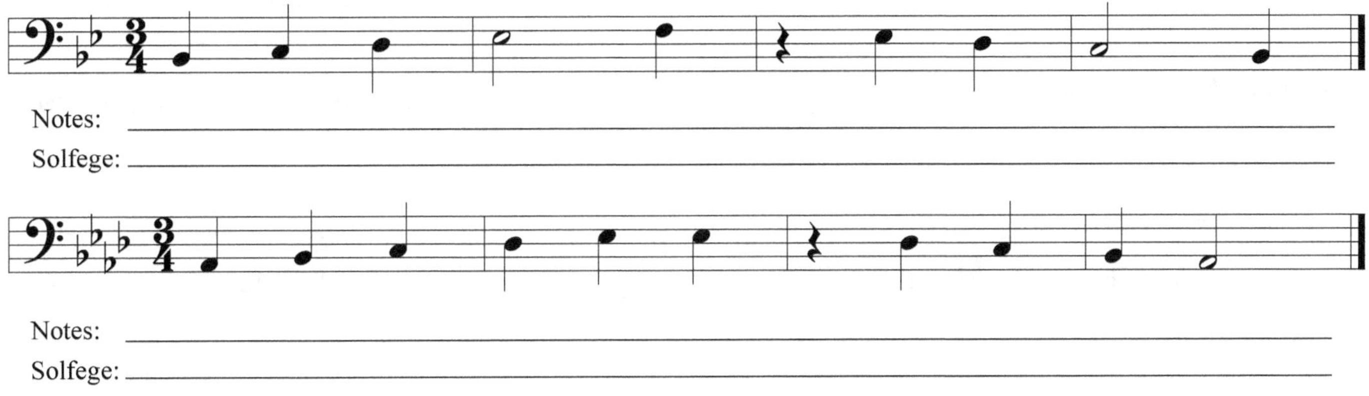

21. Check the English word that contains the same sound as the given IPA symbol. (6 points)

ʌ ___Mutt
___Bait

æ ___Black
___Late

ɔ ___Pork
___Meek

ʊ ___Cut
___Could

ə ___Around
___Bet

e ___Plate
___Get

22. Fill in the correct answer using the musical terms in this level. (5 points)

a. A ______________________ is a heavy, strong accent.

b. ______________________ means "sweetly."

c. ______________________ is a lively, fast tempo.

d. A _________________________ is three consecutive tones, Do-Mi-Sol

e. A time signature in which the basic beat can be divided by two is called

____________________________.

23. For the following questions about Bach & Beethoven, write the correct word or composer in the space provided. (5 points)

a. Bach had __________________________ children.

b. This composer was never married.____________________________

c. This composer never played a piano because they weren't invented yet! ___________________

d. Beethoven suffered from__________________________ when he composed some of his greatest songs.

e. Bach wrote vocal hymns/chorales for the __________________________ Church.

Final Score:__________/109

answer key begins on the next page

Level 3 Review Test: Answers

Answer the questions about the following musical example. (16 points)

1. What Major key is this song in? A♭ Major

2. What is the tempo for this song? (give the meaning of the word) slow

3. Which measure has a diminuendo in it? 3

4. How many times should this song be sung? twice

5. Which two measures contain a crescendo? 2 & 5

6. How many beats are in each measure of this song? 3

7. How many slurs are in the song? 4

8. Which measure has a natural? 7

9. Give the value of the circled note in measure 1. 1 1/2 beats

10. Give the value of the circled note in measure 7. 1/2 beat

11. Name the missing solfege for m.5. Do Re Mi Fa Sol

12. Name the following notes. (16 points)

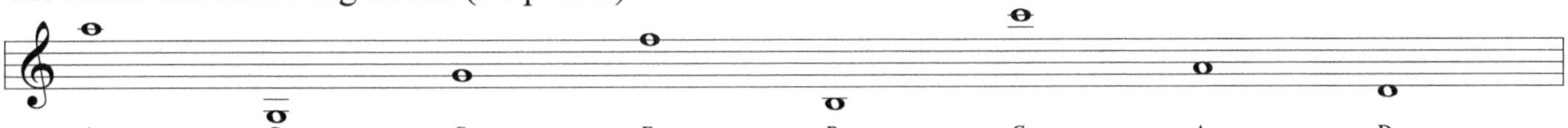

A G G F B C A D

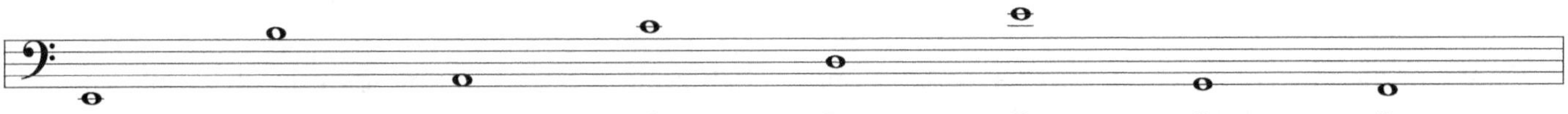

E B A C D E G F

13. Name the following notes and their values *(for example: Quarter note, 1 beat)*. (12 points)

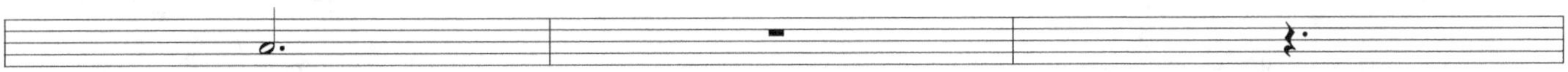

Dotted Half Note/3 beats

Whole Rest/4 beats

Dotted Quarter Rest/1 1/2 beats

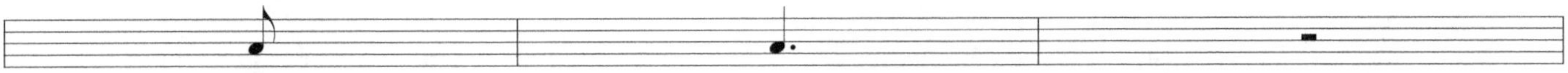

Eighth Note/1/2 beat

Dotted Quarter Note/1 1/2 beats

Half Rest/2 beats

14. Add 3 bar lines and a double bar line to the following example. (4 points)

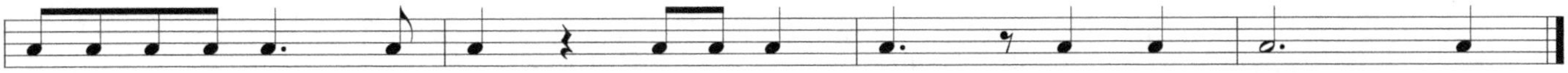

15. Add the missing time signature, then write the beats underneath the notes. (5 points-one for time signature, one for each correct measure)

1 & 2 & 3 1 2 3 & 1 & 2 & 3 1 2 3

16. Name the key signature and interval (6th/7th) for each example. (8 points)

B♭ Major	E♭ Major	A♭ Major	F Major
6th	7th	6th	7th

17. Each of these chords should have a Do (1), Mi (3), & Sol (5).
Fill in the missing note for each chord in both clefs to create a root position triad. (8 points)

18. Draw a whole note above the given note to create the requested harmonic intervals. (8 points)

7th 5th 6th 4th 3rd 7th 2nd 6th

19. Write the beats under the examples. Pay attention to the time signatures!
(8 points- 1 point per correct measure)

1 & 2 & 3 1 2 3 1 2 3 1 & 2 & 3

1 2 3 4 & 1 2 3 4 1 & 2 & 3 4 1 2 3 4

20. Write the note names and solfege directly under each note in the following examples. Don't forget to add ♯/♭ if needed. (8 points-1 point per correct measure: both solfege and notes must be correct)

B♭	C	D	E♭	F	E♭	D	C	B♭
Do	Re	Mi	Fa	Sol	Fa	Mi	Re	Do

A♭	B♭	C	D♭	E♭	E♭	D♭	C	B♭	A♭
Do	Re	Mi	Fa	Sol	Sol	Fa	Mi	Re	Do

21. Check the English word that contains the same sound as the given IPA symbol. (6 points)

ʌ -Mutt æ -Black ɔ -Pork

ʊ -Could ə -Around e -Plate

22. Fill in the correct answer using the musical terms in this level. (5 points)

a. A _____Sforzando_____ is a heavy, strong accent.

b. _____Dolce_____ means "sweetly."

c. _____Allegro_____ is a lively, fast tempo.

d. A _____Broken Triad_____ is three consecutive tones, Do-Mi-Sol

e. A time signature in which the basic beat can be divided by two is called

_____Simple Meter_____.

23. For the following questions about Bach & Beethoven, write the correct word or composer in the space provided. (5 points)

a. Bach had _____20_____ children.

b. This composer was never married._____Beethoven_____

c. This composer never played a piano because they weren't invented yet! _____Bach_____

d. Beethoven suffered from_____Deafness_____ when he composed some of his greatest songs.

e. Bach wrote vocal hymns/chorales for the _____Lutheran_____ Church.

REFERENCES

Grout, Donald. *A History of Western Music.* New York, NY: W.W. Norton & Company, Inc., 1996.

Moriarty, John. *Diction.* Boston, MA: E. C. Schirmer Music Company, 1975.

Music Teachers' Association of California. *Certificate of Merit Voice Syllabus.* San Francisco: Music Teachers' Association of California, 2011.

Piston, Walter. *Harmony, Fifth Edition.* New York, NY: W.W. Norton & Company, Inc., 1987.

Plantinga, Leon. *Romantic Music, A History of Musical Style in Nineteenth-Century Europe.* New York, NY: W.W. Norton & Company, Inc., 1984.

Randel, Don Michael. *The Harvard Biographical Dictionary of Music.* Cambridge, Massachusetts: The Belknap Press of Harvard University Press, 1996.

Randel, Don Michael. *Harvard Concise Dictionary of Music.* Cambridge, Massachusetts: The Belknap Press of Harvard University Press, 1978.

Rushton, Julian. *Classical Music, A Concise History from Gluck to Beethoven.* London, England: Thames and Hudson Ltd., 1986.

The New Grove Dictionary of Music and Musicians. http://www.oxfordmusiconline.com., 2011

www.ingramcontent.com/pod-product-compliance
Lightning Source LLC
LaVergne TN
LVHW061257100826
845148LV00008B/1153
* 9 7 8 1 5 2 4 9 1 4 3 8 7 *